STOP
TALKING
START
ASKING

27 QUESTIONS

TO SHIFT THE CULTURE OF YOUR ORGANIZATION

JEAN MARIE DIGIOVANNA

Stop Talking Start Asking: 27 Questions to Shift the Culture of Your Organization
Published by Rock River Publishing
Denver, CO

334600-0-2

Organizational Development

terior design by Victoria Wolf

PURCHASES: Schools, companies,
groups, clubs, and other organizations
for special terms when ordering quantities
or information, email
hopuniversity.com.

s book is printed in the United States of America.

To Mom, for her grace, power, and open-mindedness.
To Dad, for his persistence, commitment, and loyalty.
I know your souls are smiling wide for me.
Thank you for supporting me every day.

To Dennis + Ali,
Keep being your brilliant selves!!

Love,

CULTURE OF

10
SHARED SUCCESS
PAGE 195

11
UNSTOPPABILITY
PAGE 209

INTRODUCTION

CULTURE IS NOT ABOUT WHAT YOU DO. It's about who you are, how you behave, and how you interact with everything and everyone around you.

It's about how you relate to...

- the place you work (your environment)
- the people you work with (your manager, team, peers, partners, and vendors)
- the people you serve (your clients or customers)
- the process you follow (your norms, methodology, and rules of engagement)
- the technology you use (your tools and infrastructure)

Culture is a relationship. Culture is about *being*, not doing.

Yet in our fast-paced, "need-it-done-now" world, we have become human "doing" machines. We start our day writing to-do lists and focus the rest of our day on checking each item off. We get frustrated when issues take us away from our list because we secretly crave that shot of dopamine, that "feel-good" hormone we get when we check an item off. It's like a shot of adrenaline that inspires us to tackle more.

It's no wonder why, at the end of the day, we have very little energy for those we say we care about the most—our partner, family, and friends.

In 1989 I began my corporate career as an IT consultant at an IT education and software integration company. In 1991, I was one of ninety employees from that company who spun off a very successful startup next to MIT in Cambridge, Massachusetts. We became the ninety founding partners of Cambridge Technology Partners. In 1993 I went from a founding partner to becoming a burned-out management consultant.

It was then that I began to question what my life purpose was. I knew there was something more, so I began to get really curious and really committed to my own growth and development. I was determined to expand my life and explore what was possible for me—and that was the start of my inward journey.

I got to see how much I was doing and how little I was *being*.

I got to see how much I was judging and how little I was listening.

I got to see how much I was talking and how little I was asking.

I got to see how "*me*-focused" I was and how that impacted my relationships.

Then the light bulb went off.

If I truly wanted new results in my work and my life, I had to shift my way of being. So I started practicing *being* more and doing less.

An interesting thing happened.

When I practiced *being* more patient, I got more done in less time.

When I practiced *being* more curious, my relationships deepened.

When I practiced *being* unstoppable, I took risks I would have never dreamed of.

Even though it was counterintuitive, I realized that *being* human was the catalyst to achieving results. Shifting from doing to *being* was not easy and it was also not instantaneous, but there was one tool that helped make the shift much smoother. It is the very same tool that inspires change, increases learning and growth, and sparks innovation.

It's the power of asking questions.

You can make your teams run, but you can't make them run faster. What you can do is inspire them to think differently. Questions open up possibility and new ways of thinking. New thinking drives new behaviors. New behaviors impact culture.

As Ben Zander, conductor of the Boston Philharmonic and author of *The Art of Possibility* says, "The Conductor doesn't make a sound. The Conductor's power depends on his ability to make other people powerful."

The fastest way to shift a culture is to ask new questions.

What new questions can you ask that will shift the culture of your organization?

I thought you'd never ask!

Depending on what you want to shift in your culture, each chapter in this book provides specific questions to ask yourself, your team, and your peers that will shift you and your team from doing to *being*. New behaviors will shift your culture, resulting in increased employee engagement, productivity, and happiness.

When your employees are engaged and happy, your customers are happy.

> "Companies with engaged employees
> make 2.5 to 4.5 times more revenue vs.
> competitors with low engagement levels,"
> says a 2016 Korn Ferry report.

When your customers are happy, the impact to your bottom line is a win/win/win for you, your organization, and your stakeholders.

HOW CAN POWERFUL QUESTIONS SHIFT YOUR CULTURE?

There are many types of questions you could ask to help shift your culture, but not all of them are powerful. What do I mean by powerful? A powerful question does one of two things. It either forwards the action or deepens the learning.

The most powerful questions are open-ended (beyond a yes or no answer), and they generally start with "What" or "How." Sometimes, they can start with "Why" as long as the questions seek to understand, not judge, a process or approach. For example, "Why is this important to you?" is a powerful question. "Why did you do it this way?" is not so powerful since it puts the recipients on the defense. Instead of being expansive, it keeps them in their heads, analyzing, or it has them stuck in the past, analyzing.

"When," "Where," and "Which" questions provide facts. They are informative but not powerful. The questions in each chapter are powerful questions that are meant to open up and expand your thinking.

HOW TO USE THE BOOK

Of course you can absolutely read the book from front to back, and I encourage you to do that so you

5

have an idea of what is covered. The book is also meant to be a quick resource when you are looking to shift a specific area of your culture.

For example, if you would like to foster more accountability, curiosity, or collaboration, simply go to that chapter to learn how, and you'll get specific questions and tips to experiment with. The chapters can be easily referenced using the outer spine of the book.

There are two types of questions you may see in each chapter. One is a question you may ask others and have a dialogue with. The other is a type of inquiry.[1] An inquiry is a deeper question that you ask yourself to learn more about who you are. For example, "What is it to trust?" Each time you ask yourself the question, new answers may come in. When you dwell in the inquiry, new insights become available that inspire you to shift behavior and ultimately shift your actions.

I invite you to treat this book like an experiment. To start your experiment, pick a chapter with a behavior you would like to foster more of in your culture. When you get to the section "Now it's Your Turn", there will be several **key questions** to focus on to develop that type of culture in your organization. This icon will indicate the key questions: Some chapters will include additional questions and tips to help you go deeper. I encourage you to pick one to three questions to commit to asking each week for several weeks.

Shifting from doing to *being* takes time.

The more you focus on those questions over the course of a month, the greater the shift you and your team will experience. Give yourself the permission to dwell in one area for two to four weeks. Refrain from jumping to a new chapter before you have experimented with the questions in the chapter you are on.

Are the questions in these chapters the *only* questions that help instill the kind of culture you want? No. But here's what I know from having delivered leadership training and coaching programs for over two decades: **Less is more.**

I'm not interested in packing a book full of so much information that you feel like you are drinking from a fire hose. I know where that leads. You freeze and take no action. I am interested in you taking immediate action to create the shifts you are looking for. Not next week or next month or next year, but tomorrow.

I have highlighted the **key questions** that will create the greatest shift in the least amount of time. Think of the 80/20 rule; the questions in these chapters will address 80 percent of the kind of changes organizations want to make.

This book is part of "The Renaissance Leadership™ Series," which is based on a body of work I have developed called Renaissance Leadership™ and Renaissance

Cultures™. You may see references to the work throughout the chapters. There will be future books and resources in the series to deepen your learning in leadership and culture.

I encourage you to keep a notebook or journal to capture the questions you are asking, the answers you are getting, and what you are learning along the way so that you and your team can continue to grow and shift.

Or you can download the fill-in-the-blank worksheets and join our LinkedIn community to share your learning, raise challenges and get your questions answered.

JOIN OUR LINKEDIN COMMUNITY AT:
LinkedIn.com/groups/12309555

DOWNLOAD THE WORKSHEETS AND RESOURCES AT:
stoptalkingstartaskingresources.com

MY ONE REQUEST

What I share in these pages is my truth and my experience. It might not be your truth or your experience, and that's OK. The only request I make is that you stay open to the information, try it out, and experience it for yourself. That is truly the only way you will know if it works.

I look forward to having you experiment with these questions with your team members, your colleagues, and your organization. But most of all, commit to doing it for yourself because in the end the only way to achieve different results is to shift who *you* are.

HERE'S TO SHIFTING YOUR CULTURE ONE QUESTION AT A TIME.

ABOUT THE RENAISSANCE LEADERSHIP™ SERIES

We are living in a time of rebirth, when organizations need to think and work differently. The status quo is not working anymore. That is why I have developed a body of work called Renaissance Leadership™ and Renaissance Culture™. Drawing from the qualities and unique talent of the leaders of that time and the innovation that influenced that period, this body of work helps organizations develop cultures that honor all of the individual, cultures that consistently innovate, and cultures that ask the questions no one is asking. These times are calling for a deeper way of leading. If we do not shift, we will not stay competitive in the twenty-first century.

This first book was inspired by the first of the five Renaissance Leadership™ Principles: "Stop talking. Start asking." I reference the other Renaissance Leadership™ principles throughout the book as it relates to the respective chapters. Stay tuned for future books, resources, and mobile apps from the Renaissance Leadership™ Series.

You can learn more about my keynote speaking and leadership programs on Renaissance Leadership™ and Renaissance Cultures™ at jeanmariespeaks.com.

CHAPTER

1

ACCOUNTABILITY

CULTURE OF
ACCOUNTABILITY

WE ALL KNOW WHAT ACCOUNTABILITY IS. We know that it's incredibly important to hold others accountable, yet it continues to be the biggest thorn in our side. One of the biggest reasons deadlines are missed and projects fail is lack of accountability. It causes frustration in leaders today and ultimately impacts the greatest contributing factor that makes or breaks a team: trust.

When there is no trust, there is no team.

I can't tell you a team I have not worked with where accountability was not an issue.

Why? Because it requires having to tell your team

what to do and then having to make sure they do it. How much fun is that?

We talk about holding others accountable, but can you ever really hold someone else accountable? No, and therein lies the irony and the challenge. As leaders, we think we can, but the reality is our people need to hold themselves accountable, and we are there to support them in ensuring that happens.

The challenge is how to get them to be accountable.

Like most things we dread having to do, instead of addressing it right away, we keep moving it down our to-do list, hoping it will eventually take care of itself. Then we wonder why our deadlines slip, our projects fail, and we feel like a tyrant when we have to follow up.

It's not surprising to learn that only 40 percent of employees surveyed by Gallup strongly agree that their manager holds them accountable for their performance goals.[2]

I get it. I had the same issue holding my teams accountable, and over time, it takes a toll. The frustration with having to constantly follow up would drain the energy out of me, leaving nothing left for the things I needed to do.

I got tired of seeing this same issue drain the heck out of my clients. I was determined to crack the nut on this, so I began to develop a three-question process that shifts the responsibility from you, the leader, and puts it on the one that you are holding accountable.

I started implementing the process and began to see positive results.

But there is one caveat. (I know, just when you thought it was easy.) If you truly want the process to work, and work surprisingly well, you have to ask the three questions in the exact order and exactly as is. Yes, I'm getting a bit anal here, but no matter how much I stressed in my programs that the proof is in the process, I would inevitably find leaders wanting to alter the questions a bit or not ask them in the exact order or skip one. And then they would wonder why the process didn't work.

It's funny how our pesky minds like to operate.

Let me share the three-question process, why it works, and a fun and easy way to remember it on a daily basis. And then we'll look at how to increase that 40 percent so that your people are being held accountable and you feel more like their leader versus their nagging mother-in-law.

THREE-QUESTION PROCESS TO FOSTER ACCOUNTABILITY

At the end of every conversation that requires action to be taken, ask these three questions:

1. What will you **T**ake on and by when?
2. How do you want to be held **A**ccountable?
3. If you don't do what you say you will, how do you want me to **B**e?

As you look at these questions, where is the attention?

Yup, it's over there on the person you are holding accountable. You are not telling that person how to be accountable. That person is telling you how he or she wants to be held accountable. This is what it means to leave *the other* with the T.A.B, an acronym to remember the questions by. (I didn't think you wanted to get stuck with it.)

Once you get answers to these three questions, the accountability is set up. Think of accountability as a form of expectation setting that provides clarity to your team. Your team members want clarity. Clearly stated expectations minimize the unknown and get your teams into action. Holding others accountable provides that clarity, and these three questions have *them* set up the consequences, not you. The questions enable *them* to take responsibility for being accountable.

One of my clients was extremely skeptical when he learned the questions in my training program, but I urged him to trust the process and try it out. In our next one-on-one session, he shared how surprised he was that it had worked. Not only that, he commented on how it took more of the pressure off of him. He used this process with a direct report who was continuing to miss deadlines. His direct report would get motivated at the start of the project, but that motivation soon declined, resulting in missed deadlines. When my client got to the last question, his direct report responded, "If I don't do it, you can fire me."

Now, I know this example is extreme, but what I want you to get here is that his direct report said it, not him (even though my client was thinking it).

Believe it or not, people want to be held account-able, and deep down inside they know that it's their responsibility if they don't cut the mustard. Even millennials want to be held accountable, but they need to have a clear understanding of what they are being held accountable for and why.

Craig Hickman and Mattson Newell of Partners in Leadership have conducted studies in workplace accountability and share this as it relates to millennials: "Understanding the 'why' behind an organization's priorities, goals, or key results is crucial for millennials. They must be able to make sense of what they do, how they behave, and who they impact. When they do, they become valuable contributors who tenaciously monitor their connectedness to, and accountability for, what matters most."[3]

It is critical, when you ask the first two questions in the three-question process, to ensure the recipient's answers are aligned with what you need to hold them accountable for. And, they understand how the actions they are being held accountable for directly impact the end result.

It is the last question in the process that causes the most angst with the leaders I work with. The pushback I frequently get is this: "Why would I ask a question that assumes they won't do it before they even take it on? Aren't I then assuming they won't do it?"

No. And herein lies the issue with accountability today. We don't like having to confront missed deadlines, project failures, or poor performance because it's hard. And now I'm asking you to talk about how to deal with those problems before they even happen.

Would you rather know up-front how to deal with something when it comes up or would you rather react and respond from a place of high emotion, frustration, or stress when it does come up? What we don't confront now will bite us in the butt later.

You can choose to pay the TAB, or they can. But in the end, the TAB has to be paid.

Like any new muscle, holding others accountable takes time to strengthen, and sometimes there will be days we just don't want to do it. Setting up structures is critical to keeping you in action. One structure I invite you to set up is a place you can easily access the three questions. Feel free to cut them out of the page following this chapter and place them on a wall in your office or inside a notebook you keep with you on a daily basis. Or type them into your phone, or set them up as your screen saver. The goal is to keep the questions front and center.

In addition to putting them front and center, I encourage you to set up an alarm on your phone at the start, middle, or end of the day (just once a day). This alarm can remind you to hold others accountable. You could have it pop up as a question. For example, it could say, "Who do you need to hold accountable today?" or "Have you left them with the TAB?" Notice that the reminder is in the form of a question. Questions are much more powerful than having a statement such as "Hold your team accountable today."

Questions inspire action. Statements feel like you're being told what to do, which is why the way we hold people accountable today doesn't always work and why the percent of people who strongly agree they are being held accountable by their managers is only 40 percent.

Fostering a culture of accountability requires two critical success factors:

1. Stop telling people the actions you want them to take on. Instead, let them tell you.

2. Ensure that every phone call and meeting closes with actions *and* accountability.

How often do you leave a meeting or close a phone call discussing the actions each of you need to take on, and you end the call thinking all is well? You each have your actions, and you are ready to go tackle them. What's the issue? The reality is we leave the call or meeting and some of us tackle our actions. Others may attempt to, and then higher priorities come up. Others have every intention of achieving the action, but whether it's too daunting or they realize they don't have the support (and don't ask for it), the action doesn't get done.

You reconvene a week later only to find out a few attempted to do their actions (but didn't finish), a few completed them, and several didn't do them at all. Now you are a week off schedule. What's missing is setting up accountability as soon as you identify the action.

An action without discussing accountability is like saying the action is "nice to do."

Action + Accountability = Results.

One without the other is simply hoping it will happen. Next time you request an action from another. Don't get left with the TAB. Instead, ask the three-question process for accountability. Yes, it takes more time and takes extra effort to remember to ask the questions, but the time and effort far outweigh the cost of project overruns, missed deadlines, and time to market.

The more you close every phone call and meeting with these questions, the more it will become a natural way for you to lead. You may even notice yourself feeling lighter because you are shifting the responsibility. Team members appreciate being held accountable for what they say they will do.

If you are skeptical about asking the three questions, good. I want you to be skeptical until you try them out. But don't discount them until you have asked the questions—as is and in the order they are presented. If every leader in your organization took these questions on, the culture of accountability would shift.

NOW IT'S YOUR TURN

ACCOUNTABILITY

1. Are you willing to try the three-question accountability process out on the job and not get stuck with the TAB?

    What will you **T**ake on and by when?

    How do you want to be held **A**ccountable?

    If you don't do what you say you will, how do you want me to **B**e?

2. Did you say yes? Woo-hoo! Who will you be meeting with, speaking with, or connecting with this coming week where you can try out the three questions? (Fill out the table below with specifics.)

ACCOUNTABILITY TABLE

WHO ARE YOU MEETING?	FOR WHAT REASON?	WHEN? DAY & TIME

If it wasn't for reminders I setup in my phone, I wouldn't get all the things I need to get done. If you can relate, I invite you to place a reminder in your online calendar or app with one of these two questions to pop up: "Who do you need to hold accountable today?" or "Have you left them with the TAB?" Set it up with a reminder that works best for you. The goal is to remember to ask the three questions.

3. The language of the three-question process for accountability is important. Write the three questions down in a place you can access quickly when you are in a meeting or cut them out in the page following this chapter and place them on a wall in your office. (These questions and many more will be in a mobile app in the future

so you can access them at your fingertips. To be notified of the mobile app launch date, go to stoptalkingstartaskingapp.com)

4. Try out the questions. Be sure that what the recipient is choosing to take on and be accountable for is aligned with what you, as their leader or manager need them to accomplish. Think of this like an experiment in which your goal is to track what you learn each time so you can continue to improve. Over time, the questions will become a natural part of how you lead.

5. If you are not willing to try out these questions right now, that's OK. I invite you take some time instead to explore these questions:

- What's the biggest thing stopping you from trying this out? And why?

- What part of the process or questions feels hard, too constraining, or ridiculous? And why?

- What would you need to give up or let go of to be willing to experiment with the three questions?

- What if you tried the questions out, and it didn't matter how the process went?

I would love to hear your experience. If you'd like to engage with others who are also using these tools, join our LinkedIn community. Here you can share your learning, bring up challenges, and get your questions answered.

ACCOUNTABILITY

JOIN OUR LINKEDIN COMMUNITY AT:
LinkedIn.com/groups/12309555

DOWNLOAD THE WORKSHEETS AND RESOURCES AT:
stoptalkingstartaskingresources.com

PRACTICE MAKES PROGRESS.
ONE QUESTION AT A TIME.

**DON'T GET STUCK
WITH THE TAB:**

1. **WHAT WILL YOU T̲AKE
   ON AND BY WHEN?**

2. **HOW DO YOU
   WANT TO BE HELD
   A̲CCOUNTABLE?**

3. **IF YOU DON'T DO
   WHAT YOU SAY YOU
   WILL, HOW DO YOU
   WANT ME TO B̲E?**

JEANMARIESPEAKS.COM

CHAPTER

ACKNOWLEDGMENT

CULTURE OF
ACKNOWLEDGMENT

IN TODAY'S RAPID-PACED ENVIRONMENT, where deadlines are shorter, priorities are constantly changing, and we are forced to do more with less, we often push aside one of the most critical opportunities we have as leaders. That's the opportunity to recognize others for the contributions they make. The old adage "No news is good news" does not work in today's work environment.

Now, more than ever, our workforce needs and wants feedback, and they want it timely and often. They want to know how they are doing and what they can tweak to be better. They need to feel valued and know that their contributions and effort and time matter. This is especially important with millennials.

"Millennials crave a sense of purpose and want to feel engaged at work; while this is a subjective feeling, it's relatively easy to instill. Businesses have to make workers feel like their work truly matters, and that they're working toward a worthwhile goal. In fact, this can result in a competitive advantage over the majority of businesses; only 29 percent of millennials currently feel like they're 'engaged' at their jobs."[4] If millennials don't feel valued, they won't stick around.

One of the basic needs we have as human beings is the need to feel heard and seen. While it feels incredibly important to us, it's not in our nature to directly ask for recognition when we need it.

As leaders, we understand the value of recognition. We know it directly impacts employee motivation, employee engagement, and career development, but knowing it and applying it are two different things, especially when we have a full plate. Let's face it; many of us are figuring out how to do this on the fly. We have not been taught how to recognize others in a way that makes a difference for them. It's not something we learned in school.

Between the challenge with time constraints and the lack of sheer know-how, it's not getting done.

What we do instead is we say, "Good job," "Nice work," and "Thank you so much for staying late."

We believe it is a form of recognition because it's how we've been recognized. But it's not. Those statements are simply compliments, which is no different than saying, "Nice shirt." A compliment is nice, but it doesn't inspire action. It falls short because we are pointing to what they accomplished. We are not honoring what it took to accomplish it. This is where the true value of acknowledgment lies.

A true acknowledgment recognizes who the other person is *being*, not just what that person has done. For example, you might say, "It took courage to speak up for yourself in that meeting" or "I admire your determination to come in early every day this week so you could get a kick-start on the new project."

When employees hear phrases that acknowledge who they are, they're more inspired to demonstrate those qualities in the future. That type of acknowledgment gives them something to sink their teeth into. As a result, they will produce great things because their worth is not attached to the result (what they did). It's attached to the behavior or attitude that helped achieve that result (who they are).

> **True acknowledgment highlights *being*, not doing.**

In today's marketplace, attitude is king. You can have the most skilled expert on your team, but if their

ACKNOWLEDGMENT

attitude (who the they are being) does not align with what's needed for the job (what the they are doing), that "expert" will become the biggest nightmare for you and your team.

What will it take to move from complimenting to acknowledging?

What if you stopped and took the time to acknowledge individuals on your team not just for what they did but what it took for them to do it? How might they respond differently and as a result perform differently? What new results might you see?

Acknowledgment is not a box to check off a to-do list. Yes, it's extremely important to acknowledge your team and those you work with. But if you say to yourself at the end of the week, "Dang I haven't acknowledged anyone this week," and then you scramble to dig up something that feels mediocre to deliver, you are wasting your time. If you find yourself acknowledging because you know you should or because it's been a while since you have, it is not genuine.

We have all experienced that manager pretending to be grateful and going through the motions. It's almost embarrassing to hear such a manager. The energy behind his or her words sends a singular message: "I don't really care." People feel that energy whether they are conscious of it or not.

Don't be that leader. If you are struggling with something genuine to say, read ahead to the chapter on diversity. It will give you tools to uncover and honor your team's gifts and talents that you can genuinely acknowledge them for.

If, after you check out the questions and example phrases ahead and you are still unsure of what to acknowledge in your team member, you can always ask that team member this:

> **What would you like most to be acknowledged for? And how?**

Why waste your time wondering? By asking, you find out exactly what they like. Now, you've got a place to start.

Like any new muscle, the muscle of acknowledgment takes time to strengthen. It doesn't happen overnight. You strengthen it by experimenting to see what works and what doesn't. Keep what works. Throw out what doesn't. What is most critical is *that* you acknowledge and that you acknowledge consistently.

The more you genuinely acknowledge, the more it will start to become a natural way that you lead. Fostering a culture of acknowledgment is not only powerful; it's critical to the health and well-being of your team and those you work with.

Employees who are appreciated for who they are will be more engaged, more productive, and more content. Happy employees create happy customers. Happy employees also create happy leaders.

ACKNOWLEDGMENT

Go forth, acknowledge your team members, and inspire them to greatness!

Explore the process and questions ahead to keep the practice of acknowledgment alive for you on a weekly basis. If you'd like more support, you can explore our LinkedIn community to get your questions answered, bring up challenges, and share best practices and download the worksheets and additional resources.

JOIN OUR LINKEDIN COMMUNITY AT:
LinkedIn.com/groups/12309555

DOWNLOAD THE WORKSHEETS AND RESOURCES AT:
stoptalkingstartaskingresources.com

NOW IT'S YOUR TURN

Let's put this into action so you can start to practice the skill of acknowledgment.

IDENTIFY WHAT TO ACKNOWLEDGE

Think about one person on your team you would like to acknowledge this week. Pick a question ahead to help uncover what to acknowledge.

1. Think of a skill that he or she has acquired or a recent accomplishment achieved. What did it take to acquire that skill or achieve that accomplishment? You are uncovering a way of *being* (for example, courage, risk, patience, generosity, determination, open-mindedness, deep listening, trust, creativity, honoring their truth, passion, standing in their power).

2. What decisions has he or she recently made that you could acknowledge? What did it take to make that decision?

3. Has he or she demonstrated confidence in handling something recently? If so, how?

When you can't think of something to acknowledge in the moment, or from the past, you can always acknowledge capabilities and potential you see based on past performance. These two questions below will help.

 1. What potential might you acknowledge?

2. What do you believe he or she is capable of achieving?

ACKNOWLEDGMENT

As a recap, if you are unsure of what to acknowledge, you can always ask this question:

 What would you like most to be acknowledged for? And how?

SCRIPT OUT THE ACKNOWLEDGEMENT

Now, let's turn your acknowledgment into something you can deliver. Here are example phrases to help get you started. Review the phrases and feel free to use one that is best suited to kick-start your acknowledgment. Script it out by using the phrase, or come up with your own phrase.

Example phrases to kick-start your acknowledgment:

- Who you are is . . .
- You took a big risk by . . .
- You took a stand for . . .
- What I know about you is . . .
- What I see in you is . . .
- What I see possible for you is . . .
- I acknowledge your commitment to . . .
- It took courage to . . . (insert way of being)

DELIVER THE ACKNOWLEDGMENT

The best time to acknowledge your team members is when they have recently accomplished something or acted in a positive way, or soon after. It is also great to acknowledge consistent actions or behaviors. If you've seen a team member do something consistently, then take the time at the next major milestone or checkpoint to acknowledge him or her for that. Don't wait too long.

While acknowledging is critical, there is no formula for how often to acknowledge others for their contributions. If this is something you don't do consistently, I highly recommend putting reminders in your phone or calendar so you take time once a week or once or twice a month to script out acknowledgments and then deliver them. Have your reminder pop up with a question for example: "Who can you acknowledge this week?" Questions are much more powerful than statements such as "Acknowledge one person this week" because who wants to be told what to do?

Keep a journal of the acknowledgments you've given to your team, peers, partners, and clients so you can reflect back when it comes time for performance review. You will be glad you tracked it over time since it will make writing annual reviews less tedious.

Acknowledging others is like watering the seeds of greatness. Every time you acknowledge another, they are inspired to grow stronger and make a greater impact.

ACKNOWLEDGMENT

It's not only what they need. It's what we all deserve as human beings.

**PRACTICE MAKES PROGRESS.
ONE QUESTION AT A TIME.**

TRUE ACKNOWLEDGMENT RECOGNIZES NOT JUST WHAT ANOTHER HAS DONE, BUT WHO THEY HAD TO *BE* TO GET IT DONE.

JEANMARIESPEAKS.COM

CHAPTER

3

AUTHENTICITY

CULTURE OF
AUTHENTICITY

WHEN I WAS EIGHT YEARS OLD, I was quite the consummate liar. It was a phase I went through (thankfully), but nevertheless, I got the big fat lesson one morning when my mother wouldn't let me and my four brothers leave the kitchen table for school until the truth came out. You didn't miss school in our family unless you were on your deathbed, so the pressure was on.

Let me give you the backstory. My mother had a sweet tooth, but my parents didn't want us kids to have a lot of sugar, so she would hide her sweets in the deep corners of the kitchen cupboards. Of course we knew exactly where they were, but we made sure that if we took something, it wasn't the last one in the package or bag so as not to be noticed. My low blood sugar got the best of me, and I took the last Twix bar one afternoon. God that tasted so good!

I didn't want to be left with the evidence, so I put the candy wrapper in a garbage can in my brother's bedroom. As soon as she noticed the last candy bar gone, she went on a rampage. She looked in each of our rooms and finally found the wrapper. She quickly lit into my brother, but he swore he did not do it. That's what brought us all to the kitchen table, where we remained glued until the truth came out.

I can remember that morning vividly. I was sweating inside. It was one thing to hide the evidence and not tell the truth after my brother swore he didn't do it. But to have the added pressure of being responsible for my brothers missing school was too unbearable to take. The pressure got to me and I finally broke down and started crying. Through the tears, I told her I had done it. She quickly let my brothers go, sat me on our stairwell and in a calm and firm voice told me the story of the boy who cried wolf. That story, along with my father's Sicilian demeanor ensuring I wouldn't lie again, made such a strong impression that I am one of the worst liars to this day. (I still remember that story every time I see a Twix bar.)

AUTHENTICITY

Honesty is one of the top values I was raised with, so much so that I can smell inauthenticity a mile away. It's such a strong value of mine that I can't go too long without speaking my truth; otherwise it will show up in my body as headaches and upset.

Being authentic is not just about being honest. It's about speaking your truth when something does not align with you. It's also about challenging other people's views no matter how different they may be. Unfortunately, speaking up and sharing our views and beliefs is not a skill we are born with. Speaking up can put us in a vulnerable and very uncomfortable position, especially when we are unsure our voice will be truly heard.

When I worked in Stockholm, Sweden for a year on the regional management team covering the Scandinavian region of Cambridge Technology Partners, I facilitated many departmental and team meetings where I thought we reached consensus. It wasn't until after the meeting in informal one-on-one discussions that I realized many participants didn't really agree with what was discussed. I felt like the rug was pulled under me and I was back to square one.

It was the perfect example of groupthink, a situation in which they did not want to lose face in front of their peers. Once I realized this nuance in the culture, I altered how I ran meetings so that I would be sure to hear people's views in advance. (I share some tips

AUTHENTICITY

ahead that can be used to help ensure all voices are heard when facilitating meetings.)

We don't speak up because we are afraid of getting judged. We don't want to look stupid or lose face in front of our peers. We are afraid of being rejected, not being accepted, not fitting in, or not belonging. Fear is the biggest barrier that stops us in our tracks.

The other barrier that stops us is working in a culture that does not welcome different viewpoints. Fostering a culture of authenticity is about creating a safe space for people to speak their minds without being judged.

Judith Glaser, author of *Conversational Intelligence*, states, "We join a company to make a difference, to make a contribution, to be praised and rewarded. We join a company to bring our voice to the table, and 'lean into conversations' so our voices join in the spirit of partnering with others to shape, create and Co-create the future. Neuroscience is teaching us that 'self-expression' might be one – if not the most important ways for people to connect, navigate and grow with each other."[5]

The most powerful tool we have in the workplace is our voice. A culture that does not allow for employees to freely share their views and challenge other people's views is stifling. It leads to mistrust, lack of connection, and low productivity.

Over time, unspoken words and unexpressed feelings can drain our energy, causing a decrease in engagement. By the end of the day, we wonder why we

AUTHENTICITY

are wiped out, with nothing left for our personal relationships.

In a *Harvard Business Review* article, authors Daniel M. Cable of London Business School, Francesca Gino of Harvard University, and Brad Staats of University of North Carolina at Chapel Hill state, "Authentic self-expression isn't just important because it makes us feel better: When new hires introduce their authentic selves to their organization, both they and their employer perform better. Our research shows that when employees enter into relationships with others who recognize and verify their authentic self-views, they are more likely to share information and collaborate with colleagues, resulting in greater productivity. And when employees feel they can bring both their heads and their hearts to work, innovation and creativity thrive, and customers notice that employees authentically care about them."[6]

How can we foster a culture that welcomes different views and creates psychological safety for employees to speak up without getting shut down? Without providing an environment that is safe and open for people to express themselves, we cut off their ability to grow and develop, which directly impacts the organization's ability to grow.

Let's dive into some specific tips and questions to foster a culture of authenticity so you can create a strong foundation for trust and connection.

AUTHENTICITY

NOW IT'S YOUR TURN

There are lots of tips and questions ahead, but do not worry about taking it all on at once. Pick the tip that will most empower you, given what you and your team are faced with right now. Focus on that tip for the next two to four weeks so it can become a natural way you work. Then pick a new tip. Each tip comes with one or more questions to help facilitate communication. Since each tip has respective questions, there are no **key questions** in this chapter. They are all important based on the tip you are implementing.

TIPS AND QUESTIONS TO FOSTER A CULTURE OF AUTHENTICITY

TIP 1: *Create a safe space for people to share their truth.*

Even if you work within a much larger culture that may not foster a judgment-free environment, you can create a microcosm of that judgment-free culture within your own department or team. Hold closed-door forums where people can share openly about how they are feeling and what they are struggling with, and let them know in advance that what they share is held in confidence. Set the sole purpose of the session to acknowledge what is there and to name it. Keep in mind that the first session may open the dialogue to uncover key issues, but the real issues are often not the first issues presented, so refrain from jumping to solutions. Hold follow-up sessions to continue to allow for the dialogue to go deeper. Solutions can happen later.

By holding these open forums, you not only build greater trust among your team members, but you also give them an outlet to get things off their chest so they can get back to doing their best work. It's the first step in shifting fear into transformation. Ensure everyone's voice counts.

QUESTIONS TO FACILITATE TIP 1: *Create a safe space for people to share their truth*

1. What has been taking up mind-space and weighing you down in the last month? What's been going on for you that you would like to share?

2. What stops you from speaking your truth? What are you afraid will happen?

3. What's the thing that's hard to be with? What's the thing you don't want to see or admit about this situation?

AUTHENTICITY

4. Is there an idea or suggestion you have been passionate about but have been afraid to share? What would it take for you to share it?

5. What's the thing you've known will never get off the ground, but you are not willing to admit it?

6. What's the question you don't want me to ask?

TIP 2: *Partner with your people.*

When you are creating a culture of authenticity, it's important for your team to know it's not a one-sided discussion. As they share what is going on for them, how can you help and support them? Here are questions to help support them.

QUESTIONS TO FACILITATE TIP 2: *Partner with your people*

1. What do you really want?

2. What can I do (start, stop, or change) to make this better for you? What do you need from me?

3. What is one thing, if it were present that would make a huge difference right now?

AUTHENTICITY

4. What's the thing you know you need to do? How can I support you in taking that on?

TIP 3: *Ensure all voices are heard at meetings.*

It can be difficult for some people to open up and be authentic, particularly when one or two people at a meeting take over the conversation. As soon as that happens, it creates a barrier, leaving no room for others to speak up, especially those who are typically soft-spoken. How do you encourage and welcome all voices to be heard in meetings? Here are some questions you can ask in your meetings to foster participation.

QUESTIONS TO FACILITATE TIP 3: *Ensure all voices are heard at meetings*

If you have been working with your team for many months or years, it's completely fine to ask a specific person to express his or her view or otherwise comment. "Bob, what are your thoughts on this?" As a general practice, I do not encourage putting people on the spot, but when enough rapport has been built with a team and you ask from a place of curiosity, it's perfectly appropriate.

If you are not hearing from a particular group or type of people in your meeting, you can ask them to share but without putting anyone on the spot. For example, you could ask, "How does the marketing group feel about this?" Then those from that group would have an opening to voice their opinions.

51

You can disclose what you see and then share that. For example, you could say, "I haven't heard yet from the customer service group." Or "I haven't heard from this side of the room." Or "I feel like there are some needs you have that have not been voiced yet. What's missing?"

Be really clear about the impact of not hearing from everyone. For example, you could say, "It's critical that we understand everyone's views on this before we make a decision. If we don't, we run the risk of creating a product that will not meet everyone's needs. What requirement, idea, or suggestion do you have but have not shared yet?"

TIP 4: *Disclose what you think so you can move on.*

One of the fastest ways to get things off people's chest is to disclose what you believe is going on. It may be a hunch, but once you share it, it gives them the space to agree or disagree. And it gets it off of their mind so they can be present. A colleague I used to work with who was this young, petite spitfire kicked off a leadership off-site meeting with a dozen men in their late 50s by saying, "I bet you are wondering what this young, petite spitfire is going to share with you today." As soon as she said what they were probably thinking, they could then get that off their mind and be present. She was able to be vulnerable, but in an effective way that broke the ice.

Comedians do this all the time when they get on stage. They share perceptions they know the audience is thinking about them based on their looks or demeanor, and once they disclose them, the perceptions no longer get in the way. What does this have to do with authenticity? If you have a hunch or can clearly see that someone is upset, then the fastest way to move through it is to share your hunch or ask for understanding: "You seem frustrated with me" or "Are you upset with me?" or "Have I done something to make you want to avoid me?" Once you name what you believe is there, it gives that person the opportunity to agree or not. Either way, you will at least know where the person stands.

QUESTION TO FACILITATE TIP 4: *Disclose what you think so you can move on*

- What do you notice your team or customer feeling or doing that you need to disclose? Can you name it? Are you willing to disclose it?

TIP 5: *Don't wait to tell the truth—have a "no surprise" rule.*

Is your team communicating issues or concerns and updates as they come up, or are they waiting for the "right" time? Are you doing the same thing? Having to communicate missed deadlines or failed commitments is not always easy, especially when it may

AUTHENTICITY

impact the project. As a result, we hold off on sharing the information, but when we delay, the impact is even greater. Nobody likes to be surprised. When issues arise or new knowledge comes in that impacts the project or individuals, take time to focus on how you will deliver the news. But don't delay. The sooner team members know, the faster the issue can be resolved. As I say with my clients at the start of every project, "The only surprises I like are gifts, vacations, and parties. Other than that, I want to hear about issues or changes within one to two days, if not sooner."

QUESTION TO FACILITATE TIP 5: *Don't wait to tell the truth—have a "no surprise" rule.*

- What norm can we set as a team to ensure issues are brought up as soon as or soon after they arise?

TIP 6: *Talk about issues before they arise.*

What are the top three things you know will happen with your team, on your project, and in your department? If you already know they will come up (or the likelihood is very high), why not discuss and agree on norms or processes for handling them when they do come up so you are better prepared when they do. If you talk about it before it happens, are you prophesizing that it will? No. That is far from the truth; in fact, it makes you proactive so that when it does come up, you can move through it faster, and the team can get back on track.

QUESTIONS TO FACILITATE TIP 6: *Talk about issues before they arise.*

1. What are the top three things you know will happen with your team, on your project, and in your department?

2. What process or set of norms can we agree on to follow when those issues come up?

TIP 7: *Shut down gossip before it spreads.*

Gossip is the most inauthentic form of communication. Even if it's true, it's never directed to the person who can make a difference. Demonstrate true leadership by talking to the person whom your feedback directly impacts versus complaining about the person to someone else and encouraging your team to do the same.

QUESTION TO FACILITATE TIP 7: *Shut down gossip before it spreads.*

- Have you delivered this feedback to the person who can make a difference? If not, when will you?

AUTHENTICITY

TIP 8: *Stick to the facts.*

When giving feedback we are often prone to interpretations of what we see versus reporting on the actual facts. We say things such as "She is unresponsive" or "He doesn't care about his work." While these statements may feel true to you, they are what you think is true. What did you actually see that has caused you to conclude that? It's critical to give the straight facts of exactly what we see. For example, "She did not get back to the client after the client left two voicemails and one email" or "He has left early every day this week without sharing why." Then we are providing authentic feedback.

QUESTION TO FACILITATE TIP 8: *Stick to the facts.*

- What did you actually see that caused you to come to a particular conclusion?

TIP 9: *Stop making assumptions.*

We make so many assumptions at work about our team members, our manager, the executive team, our company, and our customers. It's time to stop. Assumptions, while they may seem accurate, often come back to bite us. How do you know they are true? The only way to find out is to validate them by asking the person who can verify the information you are making an assumption about. Take the time to ask.

AUTHENTICITY

QUESTIONS TO FACILITATE TIP 9: *Stop making assumptions.*

1. What assumptions are you making right now about your team, your department, other groups or individuals, or your organization overall?

2. How do you know they are true?

3. What can you do to validate each assumption? Who can validate them?

We want the truth, but it's not always easy to deliver the truth. Fostering a culture of authenticity takes time to develop. The more you practice these tips and questions, the easier it becomes to fully express yourself.

Experiment with these tips and questions and track what works best. The more you create an environment of psychological safety free from judgment, the more your team members will open up and share their truth. If you would like more support, explore our LinkedIn community to get your questions answered, bring up challenges, and share learning.

JOIN OUR LINKEDIN COMMUNITY AT:
LinkedIn.com/groups/12309555

DOWNLOAD THE WORKSHEETS AND RESOURCES AT:
stoptalkingstartaskingresources.com

**PRACTICE MAKES PROGRESS.
ONE QUESTION AT A TIME.**

WHEN WE HOLD BACK FROM SPEAKING OUR TRUTH, IT ROBS US OF OUR ALIVENESS, JOY AND FULFILLMENT.

JEANMARIESPEAKS.COM

CHAPTER

AWARENESS

CULTURE OF
AWARENESS

ARE YOU A FAST MOVER WHO IS ALWAYS ON THE GO? Is your mind and body consistently in the future thinking about what's next? We work in such a fast-paced environment that if we are not taking action forward, we believe we are not making progress. We think of action as moving forward, but forward is only one type of movement. There is another type of movement that is even more critical to our growth. And that is moving down or deeper into learning and awareness.

We discount that kind of movement because the progress we experience is not always tangible. It can be challenging, confronting, and uncomfortable to dive deeper into who we are and how we operate. It can also be juicy, rich, and full of incredible growth that would never be possible if we were constantly moving on to the next thing.

Regardless of what you would like to improve—whether it's your own leadership style, your team's performance, your cross-department collaboration, or your culture—change begins with self-growth. The first step to self-growth is self-awareness.

> Sometimes we have to slow down and dig deeper in order to move forward.

As a leader, how often do you take the time stop and notice what you are doing, what you are thinking, and what you are saying so that you are truly making the kind of impact you want? It is only when we slow down and become more present and aware that we begin to notice our team differently. We become more aware of how people respond, react, and behave in ways we never saw before. And we begin to notice how we respond and react to them. With that new awareness comes a deeper understanding of ourselves and what might need to shift.

In the coaching world, we call this internal awareness "self-management." Self-management is recognizing who and how you are in situations, what triggers you,

AWARENESS

where you get stopped, and how to shift accordingly.

In the absence of self-awareness, cultures live at the level of EGO, where "Emphasis Goes Outward." Individuals are focused outward instead of inward. They are more concerned with looking good, with how others perceive them, and with moving up the corporate ladder at the cost of others. They are more concerned with maintaining power *over* others instead of making choices based on what's best for the organization, its employees, and its customers.

> Self-awareness puts ego on the back burner. It acts as the observer who takes the veil off and exposes what is under the surface to see what's really going on.

BECOMING MORE SELF-AWARE

How can we strengthen our muscle of self-awareness? It requires quieting our minds and observing free from judgment. But how the heck do we do that? Do I have to sit in a lotus position and meditate in the middle of my office? Nope. (But that might be in my next book.)

One of the fastest ways to quiet your mind (at least while you are on the job) is to practice the skill of curiosity. When you become curious about another, where does your attention go?

It goes over there with that person.

AWARENESS

That same skill of curiosity can be directed inward. When we get curious about what is going on within ourselves, our attention goes inward. The trick, though, is to stay in that place without judgment. Because let's face it, we are human judging machines, and the mind can be a dangerous place to live. I can tell you to quiet your mind, but that's like telling a dog not to bark. The mind is a mind, and what minds like to do is think, and some minds think nonstop. It takes constant rigor to notice our thoughts and then put them aside in that moment to get present to what we are actually feeling. Yes, I said it—feeling!

We have been so conditioned not to feel at work that we not only shut our emotions down; we actually leave them at the door before we walk in. Our emotions are not weaknesses. The mind is one form of intelligence; our emotions are another.

I'm not asking you to start yelling or crying or expressing anger toward others, but it's important to acknowledge your emotions so you can move through them. When we are in tune with how we feel, we can then choose the behaviors and actions that will most empower us versus reacting from automatic pilot. This takes a level of mindfulness and presence, and it takes courage.

It takes courage to notice your impatience. It takes courage to notice your persistence at the cost of others. It takes courage to notice when you are wrong and not

AWARENESS

willing to admit it. It takes courage to face your insecurities, fears, and unconscious biases.

Awareness creates choice. Choice creates freedom. And freedom is what drives change.

> **If you want your culture to change, it has to start with you.**

Self-awareness is the pathway to get there.

When I'm working with clients on this in my Renaissance Leadership™ Program, I give them an experiment to take on. I ask them to be what I call a "Renaissance Detective". A Renaissance Detective is one who becomes the observer of their inner thoughts. They observe the voice that is the commentary in their head. You know that voice? The one that just asked you, "What voice?" Some call it your inner voice or inner critic. I sometimes call it your "small" voice. We all have one. We are all born with one. And, unfortunately, while I would love to tell you that you can get rid of it, you've got it for good. It's the voice that keeps us safe when we are in danger, but it also keeps us small. It puts us down and questions who we are and what we are doing.

The first stage in strengthening our awareness is to observe our inner voice free from judgment. As my clients take on being a "Renaissance Detective," they are to observe what their inner critic says, write it down,

AWARENESS

and move on. At the end of the week we look at what came up. I remind them to practice heaps of self-compassion because what is on those pages is not always pretty. They uncover what just about all my clients experience. They have a lot more negative thoughts throughout the day than they expect.

We say things to ourselves that we would never say to someone else. We judge ourselves for what we have done, haven't done, or were supposed to do. We put ourselves down and think we are not capable or not confident or not good enough. We think we don't belong, and we think about how we think others are thinking about us. It's a wonder we get any work done.

Our inner critic takes up headspace and impacts our motivation, our performance, and our ability to lead. It creeps into our conversations and thinks, "that will never work" when we hear an idea from a colleague. It's the voice that is thinking, "Why aren't I running this meeting?" — or it's telling you how boring the presenter is and how you can't wait for the meeting to end. It's telling you how you screwed up in the last sales call and how you will never get a promotion because you don't have what it takes.

It is important to notice that the inner voice is saying those things to you. It is actually separate from you. You have an inner voice, but you are not your inner voice. It is outside of you. In the same light, you are not your mind. You have a mind, but you are separate

AWARENESS

from your mind. You are not your feelings. You have feelings, but you are not your feelings. I know I'm getting pretty deep here, but this is an important distinction that will allow you to move to the next step.

Once you recognize you are separate from your mind, your feelings, and your inner voice, you can notice them and then choose what to do with them. When we cannot make the distinction, we go on automatic pilot and react and respond from our ego place. Self-awareness helps us create that distinction so that we have a choice in the matter.

> **Awareness creates choice. Choice gives us the freedom to move forward.**

For example, when we lose a client to our competitor, our automatic response might be, "I'm a failure." Or when we miss a deadline, our inner critic might say, "I'm irresponsible." But are those statements really true?

What is true is a client went to a competitor, and a deadline was missed. Of course we need to dig deeper to understand why and learn from it, but what I want to point out is how often we collapse what we think or feel with who we actually are, and then we claim that is the truth. For instance, when you say to yourself, "I am a failure"; "I'm not good enough" or when you use blanket statements or broad generalizations

AWARENESS

like, "Nobody likes me" or "I don't belong" and you say them long enough, you being to believe it like it's the truth. And then, over time, that is how you define yourself. It is not true, but our inner voice is incredibly powerful. It can take over if we let it.

When we distinguish the inner voice from ourselves, we are back in the driver's seat. Awareness is key. Once we are aware of it and can name it, we can do something about it. That brings us to the next step as a "Renaissance Detective."

Once we observe our inner voice and what it is saying, we can ask ourselves, "Is this really true?" It's a variation of the simple, yet powerful, question Byron Katie uses in her inquiry process called "The Work" and in her book, *Loving What Is*.[7] When we realize those statements from our inner voice are not really true, we can distinguish what actually happened ("A client went to a competitor and why") from the story we made up about it ("I'm a failure").

When we distill the facts from the story, we have the freedom to choose what is most empowering for us. "I'm a failure" disempowers us and keeps us believing it's true. If we made that up, then let's make up a more empowering story such as this: "I can learn from this and apply it with the next client." That story creates a future we want to live into. Instead of putting ourselves down for what we didn't do, how can we shift our inner voice and beliefs so we can continue to grow and improve?

AWARENESS

70

REVERSING THE TREND—TAKING CONTROL

Acknowledging the negative thoughts and stories we make up is not always easy since some of them have been with us for a very long time. When I was growing up, I had high expectations of myself. If I didn't meet them, I was incredibly hard on myself. The story I made up was "I'm not good enough." The reality was that if I had met even half of those expectations, I would have been far ahead of most people. I just didn't see it that way.

When I went into the corporate world, I put those same high expectations on others, and inevitably, someone I worked with or counted on would not meet them. When that happened, I made it mean that the person didn't care about me, which, of course, validated my story of "I'm not good enough." Can you start to see the vicious cycle I was in?

> **Welcome to being human.**

Instead of looking at my expectations and how un-realistic they were, I blamed others and myself for not meeting them. Was that empowering me? Absolutely not, but I was not willing to compromise my own values and what I felt was right—until it started affecting my health and my relationships. I began to see over time that I was creating my own island of "perfection" that no one could ever meet, no matter what they did. And neither could I.

AWARENESS

I had to let go of being right so that I could take on being happy. Slowly but surely, I started loosening up high expectations of myself and others. Instead of asking, "What is good enough?"—which honestly felt like I was settling for a lower standard—I asked myself, "What works for me and for them that will create a win/win?" That question allowed me to see when I was expecting too much of myself or others and how to be more realistic.

I also practiced loads of self-compassion, which felt very foreign to me at the time. But I knew if I did not start accepting myself completely and not think I had to be a superwoman every moment of every day, my health would decline, and the people I cared about most would not be around.

> **You are the master of your mind.**

You get to choose in every moment which thought is more empowering. It starts with one observation and noticing at a time. Is it easy? Heck no! In the beginning you may not realize your inner voice has taken over until after the fact. Sometimes it's days or weeks later. A dear colleague and past coach, Johanna Lyman used to share a phrase that I always remember. She heard it from a visiting minister at a Unity Church in Hawaii and it was this: "It's not how often you forget. It's how quickly you remember in each moment." What matters

AWARENESS

is that you are noticing and then diving in to see what can shift.

The more you practice noticing, the stronger your muscle of awareness becomes and the faster you can shift in the moment. How do you know you are shifting? When you respond and react differently than you did in the past, when you notice your thoughts and you don't judge them right away, and when you can laugh at how crazy the stories are that you make up in your mind.

DO WE HAVE TO LOOK AT OUR EMOTIONS?

Our mind, as brilliant and creative as it is, would not be able to be a mind without our body, the incredible vessel it resides in. And, we can't forget about our heart, which allows us to feel. Ah—emotions. Did you think I would let you get away with not having to look at those?

Our emotions play a sticky role in our work in that they get in the way of us getting things done. If we didn't have to feel, everything would be much easier. (And if we didn't have to deal with customers, life would be great too, but I digress.) Let's explore how we can apply the tool of awareness when emotions get triggered.

People and situations can trigger us at work. We get triggered when the person we don't get along with asks us every morning how we are doing. We get

AWARENESS

triggered when our boss questions a hiring decision we made. We get triggered when our priorities are set but then get moved every month by our boss.

When we get triggered, our emotions kick in, our thinking goes out the door, and we automatically go into survival mode. We judge, often unconsciously, and we decide in that instant if we can like, trust, or work with the other. What we experience is what Judith Glaser, author of *Conversational Intelligence*, calls "amygdala hijack." This is a situation in which the amygdala, the primitive part of our brain, gets activated and releases the stress hormone cortisol. That kicks us into fight or flight. Or we opt to freeze or appease.[8] When emotions are high, we often lash out, unconscious of the consequences. We are not thinking clearly enough to step away and cool down first.

Think about the last time you got triggered. Who or what triggered you, and what was your go-to response? Did you want to lash out and fight or did you want to leave the situation? Did you feel frozen or did you want to immediately please? Each of us has a primary go-to response, and it is completely normal. It's a way our bodies protect us. The mastery comes when you can intercept the trigger before your amygdala hijacks you.

If you are not sure what triggers you, look at what or who frustrates or upsets you at work. Triggers can also show up as a physical response to something happening.

AWARENESS

For example, if you start fidgeting or tapping your foot or clicking your pen or feel discomfort or anxiety, something has been triggered. Our emotions and our body don't lie. If we are unconscious of our triggers, our bodies will let us know that something is up.

Similar to the exercise I give my clients to observe their inner voice, there is an exercise in which I ask them to put their "Renaissance Detective" hat on again and notice when they get triggered. For one week, they are to write down the people and things that triggered them and how those triggers made them feel. They do this without assessing or figuring out what to do with it. The first step to self-awareness is identifying what the trigger is and how that trigger makes us feel. We are in "observing" mode without evaluating or judging.

When we take the time to acknowledge how we feel—whether we acknowledge in the moment we are triggered or after we are triggered—osmosis happens. Magically, we are able to move through the feeling faster. Why? Because the feeling has been named and brought to the surface.

> When we name the feeling, it no longer has as much power over us.

AWARENESS

Feelings that are unacknowledged have nowhere to go but inward. There is no escape route. No way for the feeling to express itself, so it builds up within us. And it gets released as anger or resentment, or it shows up in our physical bodies as discomfort.

Whatever you feel is what you feel. There is no right or wrong feeling to have. Name it. Acknowledge it. And feel it. The more you do this, the faster you will move through it. As is the case with any experiment, the only way you will know if this will work is to try it out.

Once we have the trigger and name the feeling associated with it, it is important to understand why we got triggered.

There are five reasons we generally get triggered:

1. The trigger brings back an unpleasant experience from the past—either with that person or a past situation you had a similar experience with.

2. Your intention is being shot down—the other person does not understand you, what you want, or who you are.

3. An expectation is unfulfilled—we often have expectations we want met that we have never articulated. When they have not been met, we get triggered.

AWARENESS

76

4. Unspoken communication—we get triggered because there was something we should have said and didn't. Or the other person is holding back on communicating something.

5. A value has been stepped on—as soon as a value of ours is disregarded, we get triggered. For example, you value honesty, and someone lies to you, or you value freedom, and your options to work remotely are taken away.

When I was working with the founder of a high-tech firm as part of the leadership program I was delivering, he had a really hard time trusting his people and the decisions they made. As a result, he would micromanage, or he would veto decisions that had been approved by everyone else below him. This was not only frustrating to those below him, since they felt mistrust, but they also started losing respect for him, which is a recipe for a toxic culture.

It wasn't until he had a meeting with his team and they asked him how open he was to change that he shared past experiences in which he got burned several times by people who had formerly worked for him. He said that after those experiences, it was difficult for him to trust. If he did trust, it took a very long time. He let his past dictate his future, but having shared that, he helped his team understand where his behavior came

AWARENESS

from. From that place, they were able to brainstorm together ways he could give them more autonomy while working through his personal challenges around trust.

As you look at your own triggers, what do you think caused them? Based on the reason for each trigger, explore the questions and tips ahead to minimize getting triggered in the future and to eventually eliminate those triggers once and for all.

NOW IT'S YOUR TURN

Below are several tips and powerful questions to experiment with to increase your awareness as you move through the stages of being triggered (during the trigger, immediately after the trigger, as a follow-up later, and the final step). Take a moment to review each section. Then pick the section that would most heighten your self-awareness. Take on the questions and tips in that section. If you want to focus on the two **key questions** outlined in the "During the Trigger" stage in the next several weeks, those alone will help heighten your self-awareness.

AWARENESS

DURING THE TRIGGER

Increasing your awareness in the moment can help handle these situations:

 When your inner voice is taking over. When you notice your inner voice talking, you are no longer present. Stop and get back to being curious about who is in front of you, whether it's an individual or a group of people. As soon you get curious about them, your attention will shift from you to them. The fastest way to get back to focusing on them is to ask yourself this **key question:** "How can I serve?" This will shift your focus back to them in that moment.

 When you are triggered. As soon as you feel yourself triggered, stop in that moment and breathe. Allow yourself to center into your own body, and if you can in that moment. Ask yourself this **key question:** What am I feeling in this moment? Acknowledge what you feel. Name it, and instead of judging it, observe it and allow yourself to feel it. Know that you can reflect on this afterward. Be sure to take time after to do that; otherwise, the same thing will continue to trigger you.

AWARENESS

79

IMMEDIATELY AFTER THE TRIGGER

When you observe the inner critic taking over, ask the following questions to help move through what the inner critic is saying:

1. What is your inner critic saying?

2. Is this really true? What evidence do you have of it being true?

3. What are the actual facts?

4. What can you learn from this inner critic?

5. What's a new way to reframe it that feels more empowering?

FOLLOW UP LATER

Below are some follow-up questions to reflect on after you've gotten triggered so you can understand and shift in the future. Not all questions will apply each time you get triggered, but take some time after you've been triggered to step through and see which questions will help further define the trigger for you:

1. What is this feeling about?

2. What or who am I frustrated with? What am I really upset about?

AWARENESS

3. What is making me want to fight, run, freeze, or please?

4. What event or experience from the past is this triggering in me now?

5. What am I holding onto or trying to control? What would it be like to loosen my hold?

6. What intention was not met?

7. What expectation was unfulfilled?

8. What should I have communicated that I did not? What should they have communicated that they did not?

9. What value of mine was stepped on?

10. What do I most need or want that has not been requested?

FINAL STEP: CLEAN IT UP OR FOLLOW UP

There are many ways we react when we are triggered. It's important to take responsibility for our actions or inactions after we get triggered. Here are some follow-up questions to help prepare for that conversation:

AWARENESS

1. What do you need to take responsibility for? What's your role in this?

2. What do you need to apologize for? (It's OK to ask for a "do-over" or to ask to "hit the reset button.")

3. What needs to be requested and to whom? When will you request it?

4. What needs to be communicated and to whom? When will you communicate it?

5. If I let this go, will I be able to live with myself? (If the answer is no, then clean it up.)

TIPS TO STAY COMMITTED TO RAISING YOUR AWARENESS:

- As you take on becoming more aware and noticing your triggers and feelings, it's important to quiet your ego during the process. The best way to do that is to simply remind your ego that you're "trying this out for the day (or week)."

- Take breaks to step away from the situation or the environment to reflect after you've been triggered. It will give you more clarity and time to align your head and heart.

AWARENESS

- Experimentation requires experience. There is no success or failure. There is only a produced result. So, as you take on the questions and tips and practice being a "Renaissance Detective," try to stay away from judging your feelings or inner voice. Practice being an "objective" observer.

I would love to hear how these questions and tips go for you. Engage our LinkedIn community to share your experiences, get your questions answered, and bring up challenges.

JOIN OUR LINKEDIN COMMUNITY AT:
LinkedIn.com/groups/12309555

DOWNLOAD THE WORKSHEETS AND RESOURCES AT:
stoptalkingstartaskingresources.com

NOT READY TO TAKE THIS ON JUST YET?

If you are not willing or ready to try out these questions and tips right now, that's OK. I invite you to take some time instead to explore these questions:

1. What's the biggest thing stopping you from trying this out? And why?

AWARENESS

2. What part of the process or questions feels hard, too constraining, or ridiculous? And why?

3. What would you need to give up or let go of to be willing to experiment with these questions?

4. What if you tried the questions and tips out, and it didn't matter how it went?

Fostering a culture of awareness starts with you. Put yourself first, make a commitment to stop forward action for a moment, and instead choose to take action deeper. Your mind, heart, and soul will thank you for it. And so will those you work with.

PRACTICE MAKES PROGRESS. ONE QUESTION AT A TIME.

AWARENESS

WHAT IF GOING DEEPER INTO YOUR OWN AWARENESS IS THE ACTION THAT HELPS YOU MOVE FORWARD?

JEANMARIESPEAKS.COM

COLLABORATION

CULTURE OF
COLLABORATION

WHEN YOU THINK OF HAVING TO WORK WITH OTHERS, does it light you up, or does it make you want to cringe? If you have a strong streak of independence like I do, having to collaborate with others is not always easy or fun. One would think that, growing up in a large family, I would have learned how to be a good "collaborator," but that was far from the truth. When I came along, my four brothers were a bit baffled. "She's not like us," they thought. I was told they used to refer to me as a "he." "Is he coming with us?" "Is he sleeping now?" They didn't quite know what to do with a girl.

As I grew up with them, I tried to find ways to "belong," so I would be the "bat girl" at their baseball games or keep score at their touch football games but I found myself becoming more independent as the years went on. My true independence kicked in when my brothers had to babysit me. Babysitting, to them, was a code word for "you're on your own." After my parents left to go out, my brothers would wait about fifteen minutes and then go off on their merry way. Of course, right before leaving, they would conveniently threaten me to not tell our parents. My parents were shocked to find this out at our first family reunion, which was their fortieth anniversary. Needless to say I learned to fend for myself at a very young age.

Being able to do it "on my own" was my MO, and it was a great asset that got me through college, but as I entered the corporate world, my eyes opened up to see what I didn't know and the amazing colleagues I could learn from.

I had the opportunity to collaborate with some of the most brilliant consultants, engineers, and strategists at Cambridge Technology Partners. Through the client projects we worked on together, we helped grow the company from ninety people in Cambridge, Massachusetts, to over four thousand worldwide. What differentiated us from other Big Six firms were our fixed-time, fixed-price model and the rapid timeframes we committed to each project phase. With that model came intense work environments, leading to very long work hours. But from that experience, I collaborated with the best and the brightest, and we developed deep connections that are still strong thirty years later.

Had I not had that experience, I would not have developed the skills and confidence to start my own consulting business. An interesting thing happened when I started my business though. I fell back into the mode of having to do it "on my own". For several years I delivered programs independently and did not collaborate with others.

When I finally opened myself up to collaborate again, I found myself choosing collaborators who were just like me. We shared similar views, perspectives, and work styles. We also shared many of the same core skills and talents. They "got" me, and they were super easy to work with. The problem was that after we dove into developing a program together, we would get stuck at the same point of the project—that point where each of us always got stuck. It was going from design to implementation. We shared strong visioning skills, but the "doing" part was the least fun. Neither of us was able to break through our respective comfort zones because we shared the same zone. As a result, the collaboration either came to a halt or fizzled out.

While it was rewarding to work as a pair up to a point, it wasn't serving either of us. However, the thought of collaborating with a colleague who was not like me was not that appealing. I had a feeling it would be challenging—but I wanted to prove myself wrong.

A fellow colleague approached me to explore delivering a one-day seminar together on navigating career change. Both of us had done career development coaching, but she had approached career development a bit different than I had. Our focus areas were different enough that when we combined them, we could deliver a high-impact program.

After our first meeting, we were excited to dive in. After we began to solidify the different modules and divide up responsibilities for delivering each module, all went well. When we came to the modules in which our approaches differed, we could not seem to come to an agreement. As a way to keep the momentum going, I ended up compromising and agreeing to use her approach, which in the end went against what I truly believed. When it came time to deliver, I could not connect with that part of the material. Even though I went through the motions, it felt inauthentic, and I was not at my best.

After that experience, I partnered with two other coaches, but my track record for collaborating was not great. I knew if I wanted to expand, something had to change. It was getting pretty clear that I was the common denominator in these scenarios, so if I wanted to crack this nut, I had to face whatever was stopping me.

As I dug deeper, I came to realize that I was associating collaboration with losing parts of myself. If

I collaborated with another person, I felt it would be too stifling for me, and the freedom to express myself would be taken away. I also noticed how much I needed to be right or to know more than the other person did, which of course made my ego happy, but in the end I was never fulfilled. If things were to change, I knew I had to let go of having to control the process and how I was being as a collaborator.

So I took it on. Little by little, with each new colleague and vendor I collaborated with, I practiced letting go of having to control and instead viewed each of them as partners who could contribute to my offerings and my knowledge. As a result, I felt free to bring all of me to the table.

When you have done it "on your own" for so long, it's not easy to let others contribute. But I had to choose. Did I want to expand and step out of my comfort zone, or did I want to stay in a place that kept me small? That's when I remembered one of my favorite quotes: "A ship in harbor safe. But that's not what ships are built for."[9]

Collaborating is not always easy, but the benefits far outweigh the costs. I applied the learning from my past experiences, so that when I started a new collaboration, I ensured that we communicated concerns up front and discussed and set up processes to handle any issues that could arise. I was able to communicate my needs and explore those of my colleagues before we started working together. It made all of our lives easier.

Fast-forward to fifteen years later, when I began developing the body of work I now deliver on Renaissance Leadership™ and Renaissance Culture™. As I was researching more about the Renaissance period, I was fascinated by how many of the great leaders of that time collaborated. Lorenzo de' Medici, a prominent banker during the Renaissance, would gather together scientists, engineers, artists, architects, and writers to talk about how to bring back ancient Greek culture to medieval Europe. Can you imagine being a fly on that wall?

The discussion and ideas that came out of those sessions went far beyond what any of them would have created if they had partnered with their "own" people. Today this is known as the "Medici Effect," and it is a powerful example of collaboration across disciplines.

What did Leonardo da Vinci, Albert Einstein, and Steve Jobs have in common? They brought together their deep passion for the multiple disciplines, of science, art, and spirituality to create new inventions.

How often do you work with those on your team or department to solve problems and innovate because it just makes sense and it's easier?

> **What could be possible if you brought in people who were not like you?**

People from other departments or who have skills outside of your wheelhouse or who think differently from you. Those we interact with on a day-to-day basis are often too close to their own work to be able to see beyond and ideate bold solutions.

At Apple, they make it a practice to introduce engineers to artists to help open their eyes to new designs. Google holds "Talks at Google" in which it brings in celebrities, musicians, authors, and experts from various fields to stimulate new ideas and perspectives. In learning about their world, the Google personnel can see their own world differently.

RandomCoffee, a global company based in France, took on the mission of helping firms break down barriers across departments. It provides a platform that enables the matching of employees within a company with other "random" employees from different departments of the same company for coffee (live or virtual). When you simply share a coffee with someone in a different group or department, you gain a greater appreciation for what that person does and how that impacts what you do.

Hootsuite implemented the RandomCoffee program. More than a thousand employees signed up, and more than two thousand introductions were made. After sharing roles and responsibilities, the coffee drinkers very quickly found that the conversations went deeper. Employees engaged in powerful discussions about challenges, solutions, resources, and support. This is what I call "mini-masterminding." Two minds come together to brainstorm, support each other, and solve problems.

My colleague Neen James coined a term called "tele-coffee". You grab a cup of coffee. I grab a cup of coffee. And we get online for a chat. This is perfect for those who are not collocated. True innovation, connection, and learning happen when we collaborate with people not like us. We collaborate with people in completely different groups. But it requires moving out of our silos.

Most of us don't create in a vacuum. We seek out mentors, coaches, and experts who can support us and challenge us. Juwi, one of the world's leading companies in renewable energy, recently implemented a mentor project in its German office that includes collaborating with a nearby company. It matches up individuals from the two different companies to get together once a month. Since their employers are within walking distance of each other, it's super easy. What if you partnered with a nearby company not like yours and followed this model? What would be possible?

Fostering a culture of collaboration goes beyond the people you work with today. How can you create an environment that welcomes cross-department masterminding and sharing across boundaries?

COLLABORATION

I invite you to take on the questions ahead to stimulate new ideas for collaboration, mentoring, and masterminding. You and your team may just find the perfect solution to a challenge you've been struggling with for far too long.

NOW IT'S YOUR TURN

Take some time to answer these **key questions** to uncover opportunities to collaborate in the future:

 1. Who in your organization do you rarely interact with? Reach out to that person to set up a coffee or "tele-coffee." You just never know how that person or someone he or she knows could assist you with your current project challenge and vice versa.

 2. Which teams or individuals in your organization are least like you (different skills, personality, area of expertise, views)? What would it take to seek them out for a quick coffee, tele-chat, or mastermind? Yes, this could be a challenge with someone you don't care for, or have never seen eye to eye with, but it may reap rewards you never would have imagined.

Here are some follow-up questions to further deepen your ability to collaborate:

1. If you could collaborate with another company or person in the world who could impact your team's success, who would it be and why? What would it take to make that happen?

2. What's the one thing that could support your team if you knew more about it? Who do you know who has those skills and experiences (inside or outside your organization) to supply the knowledge you need? Reach out to that person or persons or someone who knows them for an introduction.

3. Who do you want to become or aspire to become? How could you surround yourself by more of those kinds of people?

4. In which groups on LinkedIn, Facebook or Meetup or at a local association could you seek out a mentor, post challenges, get feedback, collaborate with and contribute your expertise and wisdom?

The more you foster an environment of collaboration, the stronger the connections will be among your teams and across your departments. Those connections will inspire new ideas and solutions that weren't possible before. As you experiment with these questions, I would love to hear what works and what doesn't.

To seek out more support, get answers to questions you have about collaboration or find others to collaborate with, explore our LinkedIn community.

JOIN OUR LINKEDIN COMMUNITY AT:
LinkedIn.com/groups/12309555

DOWNLOAD THE WORKSHEETS AND RESOURCES AT:
stoptalkingstartaskingresources.com

PRACTICE MAKES PROGRESS.
ONE QUESTION AT A TIME.

COLLABORATION DOESN'T HAVE TO MEAN GIVING UP WHO YOU ARE. BE TRUE TO YOU AND ALLOW OTHERS TO CONTRIBUTE. YOU MAY BE PLEASANTLY SURPRISED BY THE OUTCOME.

JEANMARIESPEAKS.COM

CHAPTER

6

CURIOSITY

CULTURE OF
CURIOSITY

REMEMBER WHEN YOU WERE FIVE YEARS OLD? OK, maybe not, but perhaps you can think of a child, grandchild, or niece or nephew who was that age. How did he or she see the world?

It was very differently from how we see it. Children look at everyone and everything with a sense of wonder. They have an insatiable appetite to learn and understand. And with that appetite comes a million questions. "Why is the sky blue? Where did the rain go? Why is her hair like that?" On average, children between the ages of one and five ask 107 questions per hour.[10] That's a lot of questions in one day! If you were able to survive that period with your child, I commend you ten times over.

Why do they ask so many questions? Because they are genuinely curious. They don't judge the sky for being blue or the rain for falling out of the sky. They observe with wonder and, instead, ask why. By about age ten that sense of wonder gets replaced with beliefs about what is right and wrong, and over time they stop questioning.

By the time we become adults, we tend to ask less and assume more. As we acquire more knowledge and confidence and become known as an expert, we move away from our desire to be curious. I call this the "expert syndrome." Being an expert can have many advantages, but as we master our role and deepen our understanding of our customers and teams, we tend to talk more and ask less. Whether we already know or *think* we know, we stop questioning.

> "The important thing is not to stop questioning. Curiosity has its own reason for existing." – Albert Einstein.

An interesting thing happens to our physiology when we get curious. "When you are curious and ask questions of others, the heart connects to your brain, engaging you to open up. When this happens it sends a whole new path of neurotransmitters that enables you to connect with others," said Judith Glaser, author of *Conversational Intelligence.* [11]

When we move from telling to asking, from monologue to dialogue, we open up our connection to others. When we shut down our curiosity, that connection weakens, directly impacting the motivation and engagement on our team.

"A study published by the journal *Neuron* shows that curiosity improves learning and memory. The study found that curiosity releases dopamine, a chemical associated with motivation that is more powerful than any A+ could be at the end of the day." [12]

Curiosity is also the secret to staying present. It helps us stay open to the diversity of ideas and viewpoints of others so that we can create better solutions, innovate, and expand our capacity for what's possible.

When I speak on what it means to become a Renaissance leader, I explain that there are five core principles to Renaissance Leadership™. The first principle is "Stop talking and start asking." The second is "Honor the diversity of ideas." Without curiosity, neither of those principles would be possible.

In order to stay curious, two core abilities are required:

1. The ability to ask powerful questions

2. The ability to listen with an open mind

Curiosity is not about asking questions for the sake of asking. It's about asking to unearth value and listening without judgment. When you ask questions today, what are you listening for? How easy or difficult is it to honor the response and stay open to new perspectives and ideas?

The listening that is required is beyond active listening, which is acknowledging the other as you are listening and asking follow-up questions that align with what was just shared. The listening I'm referring to is listening without judgment and listening for what's not being said. When we are genuinely curious, we begin to heighten our ability to sense or perceive what is under the surface.

If this were easy, we would already have cultures where all ideas were valued and everyone's voice counted, but we are just not there yet. The biggest barrier that gets in the way is our beautiful minds. The creative and smart mind that has helped us advance in our career is the very same mind that likes to judge and assess just about everything.

Let's face it—we are human judging machines.

We judge everything around us. We judge people for what they do or have and for what they don't do or have or should do or have. As soon as we encounter something or someone new, our minds want to automatically filter the encounter so that it fits into some category or structure from the past that makes sense to us. It gives us comfort to know where everything fits. It's so automatic that we don't even realize we are doing it. In fact, you may be judging this book or judging me right now, whether consciously or unconsciously. You probably started judging as soon as you opened the book. Congratulations for being human! The challenge is to notice when your judgments take over and, in that moment, get back to being open.

As soon as we judge, we shut the door on possibility. We close off our connection to others. When we judge, we separate ourselves from our colleagues, our team, and our organization.

While you may not even realize it, when you judge, you deprive the world of all your skills, talents, and gifts that others could benefit from. When you are closed off, others don't get to experience your brilliance. Life is too short to not make the kind of impact we are here to make. The world needs your brilliance but how on earth do we stop judging?

The fastest way to stop judging is to **get curious**. Why?

> It's impossible to be curious and judge at the same time.

Take a moment to let that sink in.

If you are in a state of curiosity, then that's where you are. If you are judging in that moment, then that's

CURIOSITY

where you are. As Jon Kabat-Zinn states so eloquently in his book title, "Wherever you go, there you are." If you want to test it out, try getting curious about something while you are judging it. Or try judging something that you are curious about. It's impossible for your mind to be in both places at once.

You get to choose in every moment.

> **Will you stay in judgment or will you practice curiosity?**

It requires strong mind rigor to suspend judgment and assumptions about who you think another is and instead create the space for that person to show you something different.

When I work with teams to teach curiosity and how to listen with an open mind, I give them an exercise in which the team members coach one another through a real challenge they are facing. That might seem pretty straightforward, but there is one caveat. The coach can only ask and respond with powerful questions (a powerful question typically starts with "What" or "How"). During the coaching conversation, they cannot agree or contribute to the conversation with their own opinions.

What does this force them to do? Listen keenly to what's being said because when they are 100 percent focused on the other and they truly stay curious about what they just heard, then asking a follow-up question to unearth more value is a natural next step. If they do get stuck, they are allowed to ask, "Can you tell me more?" or "Can you say more?" (Those are great fallback questions you can use in your own conversations.)

While I'm challenging them to ask powerful questions, they practice being what I call a "Renaissance Detective," which involves asking from a place of curiosity rather than from a place of interrogation. Each person's goal is to keep getting curious about what the other is sharing so as to help the other get to a specific action to resolve an issue.

Not everyone reaches that outcome but when the recipients were asked how they felt during the exercise, the unanimous response was how much they felt heard and seen. They were surprised at how quickly the conversation got to the core of the issue and how engaged they were. Many of them realize they shared a lot more than they expected. On the flip side, when they played the role of the coach almost every person found it challenging. They were confronted by how little they truly listened and how much they wanted to give advice, ideas, or suggestions. They also noticed how often they were thinking about the next question to ask while their partner hadn't finished answering the last one. It was clearly a challenge to stay 100 percent present.

When we can stay curious and listen without judgment, we give the gift of presence to the other. Imagine

CURIOSITY

what would be possible if in every conversation you had, you gave the gift of 100 percent presence?

It is completely possible to do this with your customers, with the people you lead, and with the people you interact with on a daily basis. In order to stay 100 percent curious it requires asking powerful questions and listening with an open mind. That is what it means to be a Renaissance leader.

If we are to create the kind of culture that values diversity and different viewpoints, "we need to understand each other before we destroy one another."[13] Thriving cultures start with curiosity.

Like any muscle, the muscle of asking powerful questions and listening with an open mind takes time to develop. But going to the gym once a week is not going to get you ripped. I invite you to take on the questions and exercises below to strengthen those muscles regularly so that over time, staying curious, quieting the internal chatter, and listening with an open mind will become a natural part of how you lead.

NOW IT'S YOUR TURN

Take a moment to review the sections ahead to see which sections would provide you the greatest growth right now. The first section covers how to practice listening with an open mind, the second section shares powerful questions you can ask, and the last section deals with how to get more curious before, during, and after a conversation. Less is more. Pick one exercise in one section that feels doable and intrigues you. Not because it sounds interesting, but because you are excited to try it out and curious to see how it goes. Experiment with these to see what works.

If you have any questions or get stuck along the way, I invite you to engage our LinkedIn community to get answers and learn how others are applying the questions and tools.

JOIN OUR LINKEDIN COMMUNITY AT:
LinkedIn.com/groups/12309555

DOWNLOAD THE WORKSHEETS AND RESOURCES AT:
stoptalkingstartaskingresources.com

SECTION 1: LISTENING WITH AN OPEN MIND

With everything we have to juggle, it's not easy to stay 100 percent present to another, let alone keep an open mind. There are many things that get in the way of us listening to one another with an open mind:

- Beliefs we have about the other person

- Past history with the other person (negative or positive)

- Our own beliefs, assumptions and conclusions about the other person

- Our negative self-talk (yup that inner voice in our head—you know the one that just asked, "What inner voice?")

CURIOSITY

More often than not, the assumptions we make, the conclusions we come to, and the judgments we have of others are not accurate. We can never know what is truly going on for another unless we ask, and unless we ask from a place of compassion and empathy. If you have a hard time staying open to others or you tend to judge or jump to conclusions quickly, here are some new perspectives I invite you to experiment with. Pick one to try on for a week, and see what you experience.

New perspectives to listen with an open mind:

1. Instead of jumping to conclusions, making assumptions, or thinking you know the answer, what if you assumed that you didn't know? Practice going into your next conversation not knowing and not needing to be right. Instead, get curious to learn more.

2. You never *really* know what the other is going through. What if you gave that other person the benefit of the doubt? How could you have more compassion for him or her? What might you need to let go of to go into your conversations with that perspective?

3. What if you allowed others to be just a little more human, to be imperfect, to be messy and to be exactly who they are—without feeling the need to fix, change, or make them wrong? What would be possible if you went into your next conversation from that perspective?

Tips to stay 100 percent present and listen with an open mind:

When you are 100 percent present, your mind is not focused on the past—or the future. It is right here, right now in the present moment. As you are reading this, for example, you are right here with me. You're not thinking about the upcoming meeting you have to plan or the issue your customer is currently facing. Here are some tips to stay more present:

1. After you ask a question, put your focus 100 percent on the other person, over there, and listen to that person's answer as if her or she is the most important person in the room at that moment.

2. When you notice your mind is going some-
   where else or you start judging that person,
   immediately ask yourself, "How can I serve?"
   What this does is get you right back to being
   over there with the other person. This takes a
   heightened awareness of what you are thinking and mind rigor in every moment, so I invite
   you to start small and pick one conversation at a
   time to practice this. The more you practice, the
   stronger your muscle of presence will get.

3. When a thought comes in that is from the past
   or the future, acknowledge it in your mind and
   then practice number two above. "How can I
   serve?"

4. Refrain from wanting to agree or disagree with
   an answer or add to it. Instead, get curious
   about the answer you hear—like a child who
   has just seen the sky for the first time. Listen
   with a sense of wonder.

5. Someone who is curious follows up with a powerful question. If you were to learn more about
   what you just heard, what question could you
   follow up with? (Check out the next section on
   powerful questions.)

SECTION 2: ASKING POWERFUL QUESTIONS

Practice these key questions and follow-up questions to continue to improve your ability to stay curious.

Questions to Deepen the Dialogue

These two questions can be used to deepen the dialogue and move the conversation forward. They are great to ask when you feel stuck. Be prepared to listen with an open mind as you hear the answers.

1. Can you say more?

2. Can you tell me more (about the situation)?

Questions to Seek Understanding

Instead of asking "Why?" and putting the other on the defense, ask these key questions:

1. Can you help me understand (what you are going through or what happened or why you feel this way or why you believe that)?

2. What do you think?

3. What is your view of the situation?

4. How do you see things?

5. What is possible from here?

6. I don't know where to go next with this. Where would you go? (This is great when you feel stuck in a conversation or at a standstill.)

Powerful Questions to Open the Dialogue

1. When you feel the urge to tell (for example, "We need to—" "Let's do this—"), instead practice opening up the dialogue with an open-ended question. For instance, you could say, "How can we—" or "What ideas do you have about this?"

2. Instead of shutting down an idea, ask, "What do you feel works and doesn't work about this idea?" Or "Why do you think it's the best solution?" Get more curious about the ideas and why they are good.

Powerful Questions to Uncover Needs, Requirements and Challenges

1. What do you really want? How will you know you've reached it?

2. What's important/exciting to you about achieving this?

3. What parts don't excite you?

4. What is scary/challenging about it?

NOTE: Open-ended questions are not always appropriate in every conversation. Generally, when you are closing in on a solution or getting to the final stages of consensus, you are going to want to ask more directed, closed-ended questions.

SECTION 3: CURIOSITY BEFORE, DURING AND AFTER A CONVERSATION

Exercises to Practice the Skill of Curiosity

1. Practice having one conversation a day in which you only respond with powerful questions ("What" or "How"). Can you imagine facilitating an entire sales call with a potential client by only asking questions? It is possible!

2. Think of a colleague you are currently challenged with. If you were to get more curious about what that colleague really wants or what he or she is going through right now what are a couple of powerful questions you could ask? Here are some questions to prepare for your conversation:

- What judgments or assumptions have you been making about him or her? What else could be going on for him or her?

- What do you think he or she is thinking and/ or feeling?

- What do you want to know more about?

- What's the question you've been afraid to ask?

- How could you find out more?

- What are you pretending not to see about your role in this?

Based on the answers above, come up with three to four questions you could ask to get more curious without judgment. When you have the conversation with your colleague, practice listening with an open mind with no attachment to an outcome.

After you have a conversation, check in to see how you did.
These questions are great to help you continue to learn and deepen your skill of curiosity.

1. How present were you? Were you listening more to the chatter in your own head or to what the other person was saying?

2. How much did you find yourself judging, comparing, or assessing?

3. How much did you want to contribute to the conversation?

4. What did it require for you to stay 100 percent present?

5. How powerful were your questions? Did they start with "What" or "How?"

6. What did you notice beyond the words you heard? What was the underlying mood of the other person?

7. What is a hunch you have? What is a follow-up question you might ask that comes from your gut or intuition? What do you see that's next for that person?

Not ready to take on being more curious just yet?

If you are not willing or ready to try out these exercises and questions right now, that's OK. I invite you

CURIOSITY

take some time instead to explore these questions:

1. What's the biggest thing stopping you from trying this out? And why?

2. What part of the exercises or questions feels hard, too constraining, or ridiculous? And why?

3. What would you need to give up or let go of to be willing to experiment with these exercises and questions?

4. What if you treated the exercises and questions like an experiment, and it didn't matter how it went?

PRACTICE MAKES PROGRESS. ONE QUESTION AT A TIME.

CURIOSITY

WHEN YOU ARE CURIOUS, YOU SHIFT FROM EXPERT TO EXPLORER SUPPORTING OTHERS ON THEIR JOURNEY.

JEANMARIESPEAKS.COM

CHAPTER

7

DIVERSITY

CULTURE OF
DIVERSITY

ONE OF THE DEEPEST NEEDS WE HAVE as human beings is the need to be seen and heard. Being seen and heard gives us a sense of value, worth and knowing that we matter. Having this need met is critical in all aspects of our lives and especially at work, where we spend a good amount of our day.

No matter what role we play or what title we have, if we don't feel seen and heard, a piece of us can feel empty inside. It's not uncommon to fill that void with negative self-talk and beliefs about ourselves and others that are untrue. Or we might get addicted to being right, in which case we might become inflexible and put others down so that we can feel better about ourselves.

How do we create a culture where our team members are fully seen and heard?

We honor what makes them unique. We honor what they bring to the table. We honor the ideas they have, no matter how crazy they are, and we honor each of their quirks, idiosyncrasies, and pet peeves. We honor the varied perspectives they bring to the team and company, and we honor them for who they are and who they are not.

When I say honor, what I mean is a deep respect. Honor is also about allowing for and appreciating it all—the diversity of ideas, perspectives, skills, behavior, and everything that makes each of us who we are. As noted in the last chapter, the first two principles of Renaissance Leadership™ are to "Stop talking and start asking" and "Honor the diversity of ideas." It's one thing to get curious by asking new questions, but if we are not willing or able to hear the diversity of answers that come up, we will not grow as individuals or as an organization.

If all of us, and I mean each and every one of us no matter where we sat in our organization, could honor each and every other person, imagine how it would feel to come into work each day. We are not there yet. And we won't fully get there until we actually address some of the deep-seated wounds and unconscious biases at the core of our society. But, what we can do is start inside our own team, department, or group.

WHAT DOES IT MEAN TO FOSTER A CULTURE OF DIVERSITY?

It means respecting where people come from, honoring the uniqueness they bring to the table, and honoring how they operate. What does it take? It takes courage to step out of our worldview and get curious about another's. It takes a completely open mind to let go of the attachment to our ideas and allow others to have theirs, without judgment. To hold both ideas equally in a meeting and, instead of fighting over which is best, to explore how each could work and why. It takes vulnerability to admit you are wrong and that you've held a bias that has stopped you from fully respecting another. It requires confidence to stand up for someone on your team when no one else will.

The reality is we are not perfect. Yup, I'm sorry to say this if you are a perfectionist and—believe you me—I am a recovering perfectionist (well, there might be twinges of it still lingering), so I get it. At the core of being human is being messy. There is a lot to what we do, how we think, and how we behave. To put ourselves inside an organization that has its own norms, processes, and rules of engagement—and then throw in a bunch of responsibilities like leading people, hitting forecasts, and dealing with customers—it's a wonder we make it through the day.

What if we stripped all that away?

What if we stripped away all those responsibilities, obligations, roles, titles, and expectations?

And then what if we stripped away our reactions, our stressors, our frustrations, and the challenges and issues we have with ourselves and others?

And then what if we stripped away the things that make us unique—our personalities, gifts, talents, skills, experiences, and accomplishments?

And then what if we stripped away our physical looks, our skin color, our nationality, and our religious and political views?

What would we have left?

What would be at the very core?

We would be humanity in its purest, simplest form.

At the core, we are all one and the same.

We all are from the same core of being human. We all started in that same sacred place. You are no different from me. I am no different from you. Yes, we look different, we have different views, preferences, desires, dreams, skills, experience, and so much more, but what all of us share at the core is being human.

That is something to respect and honor.

Organizations are simply a group of organisms

(human beings) that come together for a common mission and goals. No matter how we are divided up and what the organizational chart looks like and what roles, titles, and responsibilities we have, we are still in the end a group of human beings working together.

Knowing we came from the same core, what would it take to respect the fellow humans you work with and serve no matter who they are, what they bring to the table, how frustrated they make you, or how much joy they bring to your workday?

There are so many ways to define "respect." It's what makes or breaks relationships; it's what many feel is earned, and when it's broken it can take a long time to repair, if at all. Some may describe it as a deep caring and kindness for another. Others feel it's when you hold someone in high esteem.

What if it was much simpler than that?

What if respect at its very core was honoring another for being human?

What if it was honoring that person's humanity without judgment and instead was coming from a place of curiosity and deep understanding? We often associate respect with "agreement" or "intelligence" or "camaraderie." In other words, if I agree with you or I value your intelligence and expertise or I like you for

DIVERSITY

who you are, then I can respect you.

What if respect was not conditional? We can disagree with others and still respect them. We can respect others and not like them some of the time. We can respect others and be ticked off at them for some action they have taken. We can respect others and choose not to follow their vision. Respect has nothing to do with a particular view or an agreement toward or a bonding with. You may not *feel* respect for another, but you can *show* respect.

> **Respect is honoring a person's humanity.**
> **We each deserve that.**

Nobody is perfect, but we can get so attached to how others should be that we can't let it go, and as a result, we can have a very hard time respecting them for who they are.

A powerful exercise I like to facilitate with leadership teams that highlights respect and deepens connection is called "admire/need." There are many ways you can facilitate it, but I give each person individual time to fill in these two sentences for each individual on the team. The participants use one index card per person.

DIVERSITY

> **TEAM MEMBER NAME:**
>
> 1. What I most admire in you is _____.
>
> 2. What I most need from you is _____.

When they are done, they pair up and exchange their answers. They then give the person the index card that has been filled out and move on to the next person. They do this until each combination of pairs has shared.

What people hear in this exercise are often things they have never heard before. They feel incredibly valued and honored for who they are, and there is a deep appreciation for who they work with. The most consistent feedback I get from this exercise is how powerful it is because it is often the first time they have had the opportunity to share this information with each other.

In what ways can you show respect for those you work with even when you may not always feel it?

DO YOU BRING ALL OF YOU TO WORK?

While we all started from the same core of humanity, all of us have experienced our own challenges, breakthroughs, accomplishments, and lessons that have shaped who we are. It's what makes each of us unique.

Honoring a culture of diversity requires honoring the uniqueness of others and all that they bring to

DIVERSITY

their work. How much of you are you bringing to your workplace?

If you want to be seen and heard and honored for who you are, you have to *be* all of who you are and be willing to share who you are. I know this may sound pretty obvious to be who you are, but as human beings, we have this crazy thing called insecurity. We over-compensate for it by trying to be someone we think we should be or we think others think we should be or we think others want us to be. Notice all the "shoulds" and the "others' in those sentences.

If you are listening to the "shoulds," it means you are listening to beliefs from the past that were defined by others. Over time, we stop listening to our own inner guidance and wisdom and instead we listen to others. In the end, we are not ourselves.

As humans, it's outright scary for many of us to be our true selves and fully express what we believe and think. It means exposing ourselves to judgment, evaluation, and bias. It can also put us in situations in which we may share something that might be held against us. As a result, we don't always share all of our ideas, thoughts, and beliefs. We hold back at times or with certain people or in certain situations.

Work environments are no different than other kinds of communities we belong to. There are norms, social etiquette, and expectations. Some of those aspects of the work environment are unspoken, which makes them even more challenging to navigate.

When I was in the corporate world, I wanted to be perceived as a high achiever, successful, smart, and valuable. That is what often drove my actions and behaviors. It worked pretty well. But if you were to ask me if I was truly 100 percent me, I would say no. I was trying to fit in and "be" somebody. I wanted to belong. Sometimes our desire to belong shuts down our ability to fully express who we are.

> If everyone is walking around trying to "be" someone else, then you have to wonder, who are you even working with?

DIVERSITY

It is so important to fully express ourselves at work. Even though it's not always easy, the cost of not expressing ourselves has a high impact. It's tiring to try to be someone else. Over time being someone else was eating away at my core values of authenticity and truth. There were times I wanted to share my views or disagree, but I felt constrained by the role I was in, or I was concerned about what others would think if I pushed back. I was holding myself back from fully expressing who I was.

I had a belief that given the role I was in at that time, I had to be a certain way, whether it was project manager or client partner, head of a service line or regional operations manager. I put parameters around what that meant I could do and say. As soon as I took those invisible parameters down and started expressing my views even if it meant pushing back, I was able to make a greater impact, and I was valued for my thoughts and perspectives. I realized I didn't need to be someone else to feel valued.

At our deepest core, we just want to fit in and belong, but sometimes we end up becoming someone others think we should be. As a result, we lose ourselves in the process. If we operate according to what others want of us, we neglect what's in our own heart and then wonder why we are unfulfilled. We lose ourselves in a sea of conformity when all along we were meant to stand out.

> You don't have to be more like others.
> You just need to be you.

When you do that, it allows them to be them.

It took me several rungs up the corporate ladder before I felt I had the "power" to push back and share my true beliefs and thoughts. I wished I had expressed myself sooner. If I had, I don't believe I would have felt the internal struggle as long as I did.

If you find it difficult to express yourself at work, I invite you take a look at where you are out of alignment. Practice stripping away what is not you and what doesn't belong to you so that you can bring more

DIVERSITY

of you to work. When Michelangelo was asked how he made his statue of David, it is reported that he said, "It is easy. You just chip away the stone that doesn't look like David." Michelangelo didn't create the statue of David. He chiseled away until David appeared. David was there all along. What "shoulds" are you ready to chip away so you can get to what you know to be true in your heart?

When you bring all of who you are to what you do and let go of trying to be someone you are not, you can create a greater impact, you will be supported in more ways than you can imagine, and others will want to contribute to you.

Isn't it ironic that we call positions at work "roles"? If we could just be who we are and stop pretending to play a "role," we would create much happier and healthier cultures to work in. I invite you to bring more of *you* to work so you can be fully heard and seen.

HONORING AND VALUING OTHERS

The other side of the "culture of diversity" coin is fully honoring others—honoring them for their ideas, beliefs, and perspectives and their unique talents, gifts, and experiences.

"One of the chief features of being human is our longing for opportunities to be valued as our authentic selves. Being valued for who we truly are makes us feel alive. We've found that when people gain insight

DIVERSITY

into their unique perspectives and strengths and can use them at work, their work engagement increases. Most organizations do not tap this power source and, as a result, do not get the best out of their employees," say Dan Cable, Francesca Gino, and Bradley Staats in an article from the *Harvard Business Review*.[14] If most organizations are not tapping into this power source, they are missing one of the key ingredients to creating a culture of diversity.

When we don't honor and value people's perspectives, ideas, gifts, and talents, they will soon feel undervalued and underutilized. If you are targeting millennials, this becomes even more critical. Millennials want to work in companies where they can fully express themselves. It's not that other generations do not want that, but it is particularly important to them. If they can't find that where they are, they will look for another place. And if they cannot find it inside a company, they will start their own businesses. They will not settle.

How are you creating an environment that values people bringing their unique selves to work before you lose them to your competitors or you lose them to the rapidly growing market of entrepreneurs?

We tend to see people for who we think they are, what they have done in the past, or what we think they are capable of. We see them playing a specific role with their skills and experiences, and we may have insight into the skills they want to grow and develop. If we only see what is in front of us or rely on what we know from the past, we are looking in the wrong place.

You are sitting on a goldmine of talent and gifts and superpowers among your team that you may not even be aware of. Even if you've known and worked with your team for years, there is still more to uncover. When we dig deeper and allow more of their gifts and talents to shine, they will feel more valued, seen, and heard, and the team's performance will excel beyond what you thought was possible.

HOW DO YOU UNCOVER HIDDEN TALENT?

By asking powerful questions, staying curious, and listening actively. When you genuinely care about your team members and want to learn more about who they are and what makes them tick, they will open up and be inspired to utilize more of their talents.

When you think of the individuals on your team, do you know what motivates them and how they want to be valued? Do you know what they enjoy doing outside of work and what gifts, talents, and skills they have that are beyond the ones they use at work? Do you know what their biggest pet peeves are when working on a team or what keeps them up at night? Do you know the extent of what they accomplished in their previous jobs and what they are most proud of? Do you know their top core values?

DIVERSITY

I have facilitated these deeper questions with hundreds of teams to help them get to know one another more deeply. I have never once come across a team that didn't learn something new, even if the team members had known one another and worked together for years. We may think we know all of this, but until we ask, we truly don't know.

In order to engage and motivate your team, you have to get to know the members, but how much do you truly care to get to know them? As Theodore Roosevelt reportedly said, "People don't care how much you know until they know how much you care."

Knowing this information increases your team's effectiveness, motivation, and engagement. Knowing this information helps you better lead your team.

When I work with a group of leaders in my Renaissance Leadership™ program, I invite them to become a "Renaissance Detective." As detectives, they facilitate these questions with their teams to learn more. They can choose to set up one-on-one meetings or facilitate them with their teams, enabling the team members to also have the opportunity to learn more about one another.

Showing your team you care doesn't have to add a lot of to-dos on your plate, but it does take a commitment to make it a priority.

HOW DO YOU HONOR YOUR NEW EMPLOYEES?

Getting to know your existing teams more deeply is critical to the success of their performance and the success of the organization, but what do you do for your new employees? How can you honor the diversity of your new employees as soon as they walk in the door? Studies have shown that retention increases when new employees are able to express more of who they are right out of the gate.

If your onboarding process takes the traditional route—in which you share about the organization, share your core values and vision, and then have different leaders from the organization present their areas of expertise and the ins and outs of the organization—you have missed the mark. New employees want to contribute to the organization from day one. They want to feel valued and not told why they were hired. They want to be shown why they were hired. The fastest way to show them is by giving them a voice.

I invite you to enhance your onboarding process. Provide opportunities that allow new employees to share their unique views, what their ideas are, and what gifts and talents they can bring to the organization. Give them the opportunity to share the kind of impact they want to make. Explore shifting your onboarding process to acknowledge their talent and where they see themselves adding value, and notice their level of engagement increase as they begin their careers.

DIVERSITY

Creating a culture of diversity values and honors individuals for who they are and what they bring to the table, and then it seeks to go even beyond that to understand their hidden talents and gifts and what drives them.

NOW IT'S YOUR TURN

The questions and exercises ahead will help foster a culture of diversity that helps bring more of you to work and helps honor the diversity of you and your teams. Take a moment to review the sections and see what feels most appropriate to work on. Less is more. It's better to take on a few questions in one section for a few weeks than to try several over the course of a week. Experiment to see what works.

If at the very least you only focus on the **key questions** in the first part, you will begin to foster a culture of diversity. If you have any questions or get stuck along the way, you can always engage our LinkedIn community to get answers and learn how others are applying the questions and tools.

DIVERSITY

JOIN OUR LINKEDIN COMMUNITY AT:
LinkedIn.com/groups/12309555

DOWNLOAD THE WORKSHEETS AND RESOURCES AT:
stoptalkingstartaskingresources.com

KEY QUESTIONS TO HELP BRING MORE OF YOU AND YOUR TEAM TO WORK:

1. Where are you holding yourself back from fully expressing who you are and what you believe? And, with whom?

2. What is getting in the way of you expressing yourself? What are the "shoulds" you have put on yourself that came from other people or past beliefs?

3. What would you need to let go of or take on to express more of *you* at work?

4. What specific action are you willing to take on to bring more of *you* to work so you can be fully heard and seen? Take that action on, and notice how it feels.

DIVERSITY

Questions to tap into and honor the diversity of you and your teams

These questions are great to ask during your one-on-one meetings to get to know and honor your team members, or they can be used to facilitate a session with your team as a group. If you are using them in a session with your entire team, I encourage you to review the questions below and pick a handful that you believe would add the most benefit in terms of team members learning about each other. It's better to go deeper with your team on a handful of questions than to cover all of them at a high level. After you have chosen a handful of questions give them to your team members in advance so they can prepare to bring their answers to the session.

Here are the questions to choose from:

1. What is the difference or impact you make?
2. What do you bring to your team that no one else does or can do like you do?
3. What are your greatest gifts and talents? What are you really good at?
4. What do people most admire you for?
5. What is one thing you love to do outside of work? What is the quality or essence of that activity that brings you joy? What is one way you could bring more of that quality into your existing work?

6. What's one trait or skill that comes so naturally to you that you don't think anything of it? How could you leverage more of that skill at work?

7. What's one fact about you that would most surprise people who work with you?

8. What is your biggest pet peeve when working on a team?

9. What motivates you? How do you want to be valued?

10. What are you most proud of?

How to Facilitate the Team Session

After you have selected a handful of questions above and given them to your team members to think about in advance, one of the most engaging ways to facilitate the team session is to place flip charts up on the walls with one for each team member. Have each team member walk over to a flip chart and write his or her name at the top and then have him or her write down the answers to the questions you had them prepare in advance from the list above. Having them write down key points to each question should suffice. When everyone is done with answering the questions on his or her respective flip chart, have the team members walk around to see the charts of their teammates and have them add their own answers based on the perspective of how they know that individual.

DIVERSITY

It's best when everyone has a different colored marker so that in the end the participants can see the added comments from their team members. Then give all the participants time to go back and read their own charts and see what their team members said about them. It's an incredibly powerful exercise to honor and respect one another. Remind participants to take a picture of their own flip chart because when they have a bad day, they can look at the picture for a reminder of who they are.

DIVERSITY

> **We each have a place in society to do our best work.**

We do our best work when we are recognized by our unique gifts and talents and honored for who we are.

When you shift from telling others how much you value or appreciate them to asking them about themselves and their views and ideas and then listening with an open mind, you are creating a culture of diversity. A culture of true diversity not only leads to better performance results and greater engagement and fulfillment, but it also meets the core need to be seen and heard as a human being.

We all deserve that.

**PRACTICE MAKES PROGRESS.
ONE QUESTION AT A TIME.**

DIVERSITY

WE ARE EACH UNIQUE. HONOR ALL THAT YOU ARE AND ALL THAT YOU ARE BECOMING. HONOR OTHERS FOR ALL THAT THEY ARE AND ALL THAT THEY ARE BECOMING.

JEANMARIESPEAKS.COM

CHAPTER

8

LEARNING

CULTURE OF
LEARNING

AS LEADERS, WE DON'T ALWAYS GET TO CHOOSE who we would like on our team. At times, there are going to be individuals whose skills may not be up to par with what we need. We may not get team members with the level of experience we would like, but if they are committed to growth and development and have the aptitude to learn, they will not only survive — they will thrive. Why? Because they have a desire to learn and soak up everything possible to be their very best.

The founder of the IT Educational Firm I started with followed this very premise and implemented a brilliant model for growth. He hired young college grads for aptitude and attitude, not always for deep expertise. If he found really smart people who had the aptitude to solve problems, the desire to grow, and the appetite to learn, then his thinking was that they could pick up the other skills they needed.

And that's how the company we spun off became one of the fastest-growing, most-watched IT consulting firms in the early '90s. We even became a case study at the Harvard Business School. That model was what created the "magic" in our company. That special sauce was often hard to describe or pinpoint because it had everything to do with the combination of people we hired.

They were committed to learning. The environment valued learning. The culture naturally became a culture of learning and growth.

When you think of the most influential leaders either inside or outside your organization, the most common traits you will see is a desire to learn, a commitment to self-growth, and a curiosity to expand their knowledge and experience.

I have always loved to learn. But I started wondering if I had an issue with focus. Once I felt I had mastered something, I would get bored and would move on to the next thing. What I came to realize was that it was the experience of learning that I enjoyed. Once I had mastered the experience, I was ready to learn something new.

LEARNING

We are all driven to learn differently.

It's important to understand how your team members learn and what motivates each of them to learn. I was not a "book learner," for example, so reading felt like a chore. I would rather sit in my room and paint all day or start an arts-and-crafts project and be in the experience versus reading about it. Inevitably I would have to do research for a paper for school, which required more reading than I liked. When I came across a word I had no understanding of, I hated having to look it up. (There was no World Wide Web back then.) Instead, I would ask my father what it meant. But he wouldn't share a thing. Instead, he would tell me to look it up in the dictionary. In my frustration, I would drag my butt over to the dining room to go look it up.

Our dining room walls were lined from top to bottom with books since both my parents were avid readers. Then there was the dictionary. That dictionary was the fattest book I had ever seen in my life. It sat on an angled shelf you could stand at to look words up. It had a stiff linen, crème-colored cover that faded over time from its heavy use. Along the outer edge of the pages were half-moon indentations with a letter of the alphabet on them. Once you found the letter on the indentation, you could place your finger there and open that part of the book. After locating my letter, I found that it took all the strength I had to open that behemoth

LEARNING

of a book up and flip the pages. And the text! It should have come with a magnifying glass. I would eventually locate my word, and all would be well in my world.

Even though I disliked having to look up those words, it wasn't until years later that I learned to appreciate his directive to walk over and look them up (or as he would say, his "invitation" to look them up). Instead of receiving the answer from him, I experienced searching for it myself, and because of that, the definition of those words stuck with me.

Today, learning has completely changed. Every piece of information you could possibly imagine is accessible with one touch of the keyboard. Getting information is no longer an issue. The challenge today is creating learning experiences that offer your employees the opportunity to think for themselves.

When you think of a powerful mentor, leader, or manager who has helped you grow, what qualities or skills did that person utilize? I'm going to guess that your greatest level of growth happened when he or she asked powerful questions that challenged you to think for yourself. A successful learning culture challenges, questions, and inquires. It allows for the opportunity to grow beyond your comfort zone.

WHERE IS YOUR EDGE AS A LEADER?

Your edge is that place where, if you were standing on it and looking down, it would feel a bit scary. It's the place where you know you need to grow, but it feels uncomfortable to go there. Discomfort and edges, while not always easy to master and move beyond, are opportunities for your greatest areas of growth. Growth doesn't happen in a vacuum. It happens in an environment that welcomes and encourages experimentation and failure.

> **How do you encourage your team to step out of their comfort zones and go to their edges?**

And if you do encourage them, what if they mess up? Our greatest learning does not come from success. It comes from failure. But if your culture shuns failure, or if there is no wiggle room for something to go wrong imbedded in the timelines of your projects, you create instead a culture of high stress. That's a culture where people are more on edge than moving beyond their edge.

Not every project has the luxury of allowing for mistakes. As leaders we need to be conscious of where we are setting ourselves up for failure versus creating the space to allow for failure. This requires a shift in mind-set and a shift in your environment. The questions and exercises ahead will help you get there.

HOW CAN YOU MAGNIFY THE IMPACT OF YOUR LEARNING?

In addition to creating a safe environment for learning and growth, a strong learning culture shares best

LEARNING

practices and lessons learned within your team, across departments, and even across companies.

The last principle of the core principles of Renaissance Leadership™ is "Magnify the impact." When we magnify the impact, we take one experience or achievement and look at how we can apply or leverage that experience across the rest of the organization to create a greater impact. How many brilliant ideas and results has your team achieved that have never been shared?

> **How could you magnify the impact of your team's ideas beyond your project and department?**

A team in a region five hundred miles away could be struggling with the same issue your team resolved two months ago. A group at headquarters could be looking for ways to streamline its sales forecast process, which is what your team just did for one of your clients a month ago. Magnifying the impact of your ideas could create your competitive edge in the marketplace today.

Not all are ready to share their best ideas. There will always be leaders and teams who keep their greatest learning and best ideas to themselves as a means to protect their turf, but I don't believe we typically withhold information intentionally. More often than not, we don't take the time (or have the time) to stop and

LEARNING

reflect at the end of a project before moving onto the next one. Even if we do take the time, we don't always have the physical infrastructure in place to input and share knowledge across groups.

Our timelines are much shorter, but there is a cost to jumping to the next project right away. When we don't mine for the learning and uncover opportunities to apply that learning, we miss opportunities to streamline and innovate.

> What kind of commitment are you willing to make to uncover and capture post-project learning so that other groups can benefit?

Perhaps you currently hold "lunch and learns" or "Friday sales meetings" or "best practices Fridays." Those kinds of sessions are a great start, but what specific actions come out of the meetings? How are you applying the learning and ideas you just heard and putting them into action *across* the organization?

If you are not applying the learning, then it is simply a nice time together. Social gatherings to share learning are great, but learning for the sake of learning is temporary. A culture that fosters learning with the intention to magnify the impact of that learning will create the greatest value and biggest return on investment.

LEARNING

HOW BIG IS YOUR APPETITE TO LEARN?

Learning is not for the faint of heart, but as soon as we stop being curious, we lose our desire to learn. Leonardo da Vinci continued questioning, discovering, and exploring topics that had already been well researched. He knew that by diving in deeper he would discover something new. The biggest reason many of his contracts for paintings ended with a frustrated buyer is because he took years to finish them. For some buyers, he never finished. Why? Because he felt there was always more to learn. While this was not what the buyer wanted to hear, it was clearly a testament to his commitment to learn.

We don't have the luxury of time like da Vinci did back in the Renaissance. Time is a precious commodity. Time is money. Leveraging your time to apply the benefits of learning is critical.

> **If learning were the currency for growth, how rich would your organization be?**

How can you increase your currency for growth so that you not only have more engaged employees, the learning you streamline and leverage could create your next competitive advantage? I invite you to explore the questions below to increase your currency for learning and growth.

LEARNING

NOW IT'S YOUR TURN

The questions and exercises ahead will help foster a culture of learning that enables you and your team to challenge your edge and help magnify the impact of your ideas. Take a moment to review the sections to see which section could benefit you and your team most right now. Less is more. It's better to take on one exercise in one section for a few weeks than to try several over the course of the week. Experiment to see what works.

If at the very least you only ask the **key questions** in section one, you will begin to develop a stronger culture for learning. If you have any questions or get stuck along the way, you can always engage our LinkedIn community to get answers and learn how others are applying the questions and tools.

JOIN OUR LINKEDIN COMMUNITY AT:
LinkedIn.com/groups/12309555

DOWNLOAD THE WORKSHEETS AND RESOURCES AT:
stoptalkingstartaskingresources.com

LEARNING

SECTION 1: YOUR LEARNING EDGE

These questions will help you identify your learning edge as a leader. You can apply the same questions to individuals on your team by replacing "leader" with each individual's role or by removing the reference to "leader" altogether.

 1. Where is your edge as a leader? That place that you know you need to grow to, but it feels scary to go there. Where are you most uncomfortable or challenged with being a leader? Where do you get stopped?

 2. What would it take to lead from that edge? Who would you need to be to lead from that edge?

3. If you are unsure of where your edge is, what would you like to be able to master as a leader, but you're not there yet? Where do you need to grow next?

4. What would be possible for you, your team, and your customers if you led from that edge?

5. What is one specific action you would be willing to take on in the next month to lead from that edge? Commit to taking that action this month.

SECTION 2: CREATE A CULTURE OF LEARNING WITH YOUR TEAMS OR PROJECTS

These questions are great to facilitate with your team to uncover the team members' growth areas, understand how they learn, and capture the learning post-project in the most effective way.

These are questions to uncover your team's areas of learning and growth:

1. What do you want to contribute? What are you here to teach?

2. What are you here to learn? What do you want to experience?

3. What are you hungry for?

4. How do you best like to learn?

5. What new learning from the past project or team will you apply?

Here are questions to create a mind-set and environment for experimentation and failure:

 1. How do you encourage your team to step out of its comfort zone and go to its edge? Is it OK

if your team messes up? How could you give your team more room to grow?

2. How do you currently view failure? How do you currently view mistakes? Do you view them differently for yourself than you do for your team?

3. How much do you allow for experimentation on your team? How much do you allow for failure?

4. When someone fails or makes a mistake, what is your initial reaction? What might need to shift to welcome failure and allow for mistakes?

5. What's a new perspective you could experiment with around failure and mistakes?

LEARNING

Here are questions to capture learning after a project or major milestone:

1. What did you learn most from this experience?

2. What new tools, processes, or behaviors did you learn?

3. In what ways have you grown and not even realized it?

4. If you had to start over, what would you do differently?

5. How will you put this learning into practice on a day-to-day basis? What specific actions will you take this week or month?

6. What needs to be updated and shared as a result of this learning?

Here are questions to share ideas and magnify the impact

1. What best practices, learning, or ideas have you found most valuable in the last six months? Who else in the organization could benefit from those?

2. What is the easiest way to share that information with other groups or teams? Do you currently have an internal wiki or knowledge base you can add information to and share with others?

3. How do you share best practices and lessons learned on a consistent basis? If you don't share

LEARNING

best practices today, what is one action you could implement to make that happen?

4. What learning can you glean from outside of your organization to apply to your current project or challenges?

Creating a culture of learning does not happen overnight. It starts with one team and one project and one opportunity at a time. When you begin to ask these questions, you will foster an environment that allows for experimentation and failure, a place where people are free to be the best they can be. You will create a culture where people value learning and are committed to continuous growth and improvement.

**PRACTICE MAKES PROGRESS.
ONE QUESTION AT A TIME.**

LEARNING

IF LEARNING WERE THE CURRENCY FOR GROWTH, HOW RICH WOULD YOUR ORGANIZATION BE?

JEANMARIESPEAKS.COM

CHAPTER

PLAY

CULTURE OF
PLAY

I REMEMBER THE DAYS SO VIVIDLY. That recess bell would ring loudly and reverberate through the hallways and out into the playground. Once we heard it, we would run to the classroom door to line up, excited to go outside. When we got to the double doors that opened up to the playground, we just about trampled over our closest friends trying to get through.

All in the name of play. With only one goal in mind. To have fun.

The playground was a sight to be seen. Some kids were playing tag or hide-and-go-seek. Others were screaming (or crying) as they went down the slide that felt like 100 degrees of hot metal on your legs. You wished you weren't wearing shorts that day. Others were on the swings having a grand ole time while others like me preferred to jaywalk in between the swings as they were swinging. (Yup, I got stitches in my chin for jaywalking in first grade, but that's a story for another day.) We climbed on the jungle gym and swung on the monkey bars and played hopscotch on our home-made court drawn with chalk. And then there were smaller groups playing jacks or Chinese jump rope. I can still remember the steps in Chinese jump rope: "in, out, side, side, on, in, out." The world was our oyster— until that bell rang again to go back to class.

How did recess impact the rest of our day? We went back to class rejuvenated, we could focus better, we got our dose of vitamin D, we released stress and tension, and we increased the blood flow through the vessels in our brains and improved our brain performance. That last piece I was not aware of at the time. Aside from the physical aspects, it was the one activity that took us away from the classroom and gave us the freedom to be.

What does play have to do with business?

Work can be extremely stressful—to the point where we can get so serious that we forget that it could be fun. But play is serious business. Yup, I said it.

PLAY

> **Play is serious business.**

Fostering a culture of play is about finding time to step away from your work to rest your mind and socialize with others. It's also about shifting how you relate to your work so that it feels lighter. And it's about incorporating engaging ways to approach your work so you can be productive *and* happy.

HOW DOWNTIME CAN FOSTER A CULTURE OF PLAY

Can you relate to growing up with this work ethic: "If you finish your work, then you can play"?

I sure did. And, while that was great for work, I ended up relating to play as the last thing I was allowed to do if I had time after the work. Finish your homework, do the chores, and *then* you can go outside to play (if it wasn't too late). As a child, all I wanted to do was play, so I was on a mission to get everything done as fast as I could. Quality was not a concern.

As adults, we need breaks to "play"—not only for our bodies to recharge, but also for our minds to rest. Our work can be highly stressful and intense. We are forced to do more with less, our deadlines are tighter, and our workload and demands are greater than ever before so who has time for play?

PLAY

> The question is not whether you fit in time
> for play; it's *how* you fit it in.

"Research dating back to the late 1800's indicates that people learn better and faster when their efforts are distributed, rather than concentrated. That is, work that includes breaks and down time proves more effective than working in long stretches."[15]

I get it. It can get intense when you and your team need to put the pedal to the metal to reach a tight deadline. I've been there more times than I want to remember, but the cost of not fitting in breaks for play can be hefty. The cost will show up as sick days due to employee burnout, which, surprisingly, is usually not caused by being sick. Our physical body is reacting to our mental stress, which gets us sick. The costs of lost productivity and decline in the quality of the work have a great impact on projects. Would you rather pay less now (loss of time due to breaks) or pay more later (poor quality of work due to sick days)?

Pay later and your bottom line suffers.

Surprisingly, the body and the mind don't need a lot of downtime to recharge. They need just enough time to get the mind off of a work project and onto something else for a brief break. Your work environment, like so many today, may already be set up with areas to take a break. Like many of my clients, you may have foosball or ping-pong tables or even a basketball

PLAY

hoop in an area of your building. You may hold social events like Friday happy hour or outings where employees can get together outside of work.

Those are all great as long as those who are not participating and don't have the desire to participate don't shun those who do, thinking they are "slackers" or "fooling around." Breaks for play are the very reason we can go back to work refreshed, with new ideas and solutions to challenges we previously struggled with.

The original head of Nissan Design Studios in San Diego (now called "Nissan Design America") was tasked with creating a highly innovative team. When he noticed that the team was running out of steam, he would send its members out to see a movie. When they came back, they were refreshed and reenergized and ready to get back to work and ideate.

It's often during downtime that we get our best ideas. It's when we are going out for a jog at lunchtime or getting a coffee down the street with colleagues or taking a walk outside. Even sitting in a nearby park for ten minutes can be just the ticket to rejuvenate your mind. Breaks allow our brains to relax and let new ideas come in. I invite you and your team to find the time to take time away from your work environment. You will come back feeling more productive, and your mind will be more rested.

PLAY

> A happy mind makes for a happy team member.

In what ways are you inspiring your teams to step out of the day-to-day routine for unstructured time to intentionally play?

YOUR PHYSICAL ENVIRONMENT CAN FOSTER A CULTURE OF PLAY

How does your work environment foster a culture of play? The Red Bull office in Soho, London, has rooms that are decorated like a living room. Some offices even have a swing you can sit on while having a meeting with those on the couch. Selgascano, an architectural firm in Madrid, has desks lining one side of its building, which has glass from top to bottom and on the ceiling. When the employees work there, they feel like they are completely outside.

The Google office in Zurich has a spiral slide. Employees can slide down and land right in the cafeteria, which is set up more like a café, where groups can convene to brainstorm and collaborate. YouTube, based in San Bruno, California, has a large putting green in the middle of a sea of cubes. The staff members can either use real putters or very large putters, or they can lie on the ground and shoot with pool sticks. How can you switch up the dull, gray, lined cubicles on every floor and enhance or update your

PLAY

176

office so that your physical environment stimulates creativity and play?

The Comvert office in Milan, Italy designs, produces and distributes clothing for skateboarders and snowboarders. They converted an old movie theater into its office space, where it built an elevated skate park that is viewable from the first level (and usable as well). Pallotta TeamWorks in Los Angeles had to work within a tight budget of $40 per square foot when building its new offices. To stay within that budget, Pallotta used containers for cubicles and cut out one side to put sliding glass doors. It stacked them up three levels high with an elevator to reach them. When you walk into the space, you can't help but want to work in one of those cubes.

"According to a recent PricewaterhouseCoopers survey, 77% of CEOs name creativity as their greatest skill shortage, so providing an environment that actively fosters creativity is essential."[16]

Is your own office conducive to creativity?

There are small things you can do to shift your office space to foster more creativity and play. Adding plants brings life to your space and can significantly improve visual creativity. Bringing in more color and pictures to your space can inspire and stimulate ideas. Covering the top of your desk with colored paper can

PLAY

stimulate more ideas than you might imagine. When you are on the phone or talking to a colleague at your desk and ideas pop in, you can immediately write them down on your "paper" desk. I bought a roll of yellow paper and covered my desk with it. I set my laptop and other items on top. Within a week, it was covered with ideas, thoughts, and reminders that I could easily refer back to and use on my projects. Once it fills up, I take a picture of it (you don't want to lose your brilliant ideas) and replace it with a clean one.

How about your meetings? Aren't they the most exciting events you have during the day? What if at your next meeting you brought in stress balls and fidget toys and put them in the middle of the table or at each place at the table? They not only would make the meeting fun, but also—for those who have any kind of attention deficit—provide a way for the mind to focus on something else so participants could stay more present.

Try it at your next team meeting, and notice how the energy in the room shifts. I bring toys to every off-site meeting I facilitate and program I deliver, even when the gathering is with groups of executives. They are a little skeptical at first, but within a few minutes of sitting down, they are picking up the toys and playing with them.

How conducive is your physical work environment to creativity and play? What areas could be enhanced or could use a makeover?

PLAY

CREATIVITY CAN FOSTER A CULTURE OF PLAY

In addition to modifying your physical environment, you can foster play and creativity by the benefits you provide to your employees. At W.L. Gore and Associates, the company that originally created Gore-Tex, each employee is given the opportunity to devote 10 percent of his or her time to creativity in order to focus on areas outside of work that are enjoyable. At Cambridge Technology Partners, the high-tech start-up where I worked, there was a benefit that if you worked there for over seven years, you got a paid one month off allocated to personal enrichment time (PET). You had to do something unrelated to work, and the company granted up to $2,000 to use toward supplies and expenses outside of your living and travel.

I was so eager to take my PET that I took two weeks of vacation before my seventh year and went on three artist-related vacations in Europe. First, I went to the south of France to learn printmaking and watercolor painting. Then I went to Tuscany to learn glass bead making. And finally I went to the Isle of Skye in Scotland for landscape painting. Do you think I came back refreshed and rejuvenated? You bet!

These companies know and trust that when their employees focus on something completely different from work, the right brain will flourish, and they will come back inspired with new ideas and fresh perspectives. They will be ready to be productive.

PLAY

In what ways are you inspiring your teams to intentionally be creative and tap more into the right side of their brains?

MIND-SET CAN SHIFT THE CULTURE OF PLAY

How do you relate to your work? Do you see it as hard, challenging, fun, exciting, frustrating, serious, or interesting? How you relate to your work directly impacts how you work and how others work around you. Nobody likes to work for a manager who is all work and no play 110 percent of the time. All work and no play can make for a very dull workforce and a very long workweek. If you tend to be that kind of serious leader, the mind-set and intensity you bring to your team directly impacts the people you work with, those who work for you, and the customers you serve.

Sometimes we take our work so dang seriously that we squeeze all the juice out of it. Is our work important? Yes. Are the companies you work with important? Yes. Are the customers you serve important? Yes. But too often we associate importance with seriousness.

What if we looked at work as fun *and* important, lighthearted *and* important? But let's not let seriousness lead the pack. Because, in the end, would you want your gravestone to say, "She worked hard every day" or "He had a strong commitment to work"? Or would you rather have it say, "He laughed his ass off at work while making a huge difference"?

PLAY

Your mind-set at work is contagious.

If you tend to see work as too serious, what might you need to give up or take on to loosen that mind-set?

PROBLEM-SOLVING TECHNIQUES THAT FOSTER A CULTURE OF PLAY

We typically solve problems by getting in a room with a large white board, and we discuss, brainstorm, and draw. In the end, we capture our findings. How could problem-solving be more fun? Here are three techniques you can experiment with when solving problems today:

1. **Problem/solutions swap**—This is great when you have several challenges your team or customer is facing and you need to come up with solutions. Use large index cards. Get into small groups of two to four people. Each group takes a current problem to solve and writes it down on one index card. Now give your card to the next group. That group brainstorms on possible solutions to that problem and writes it on the back of the index card. Have a rep from each group share the solutions with the larger group to get even more ideas.

2. **Flip chart building**—This is the same concept as the problem/solutions swap except that you

PLAY

write down each problem on a separate piece of flip chart paper and tape the flip chart up on the walls of the meeting room so there is enough space between each one. Get into small groups. Each group stands next to the piece of flip chart and brainstorms solutions to the problem that is currently written on the flip chart. The group writes their solutions below the problem on the flip chart paper. After a period of time, each group can walk to the next flip chart paper to brainstorm and write down solutions to that particular problem. Then you can share the findings as an entire group.

3. **Speed ideation**—Get into groups of two to four. For each problem, set a timer for fifteen minutes. Each group has fifteen minutes to come up with as many solutions to the problem as possible. You can keep setting time intervals, but the idea is to get as many solutions down as possible without judging or assessing.

ACCOUNTABILITY THAT FOSTERS A CULTURE OF PLAY

One of the most difficult things to make more "fun" is accountability. Getting things done, especially when the task is mundane or difficult or intense, becomes harder to complete because it's just not "fun." Here are three techniques you can try in order

PLAY

to make it easier, more fun, and more doable for you and your team to accomplish:

1. **"Get-it-done buddy"**—Getting things done on our own is not always easy. Partnering with someone else, who has to get a bunch of stuff done, can make it more fun. Find a "get-it-done buddy" at work, where you can hold each other accountable to get what you need to get done that day or that week. Commit to a consistent day and time that you will check in to tell each other what you plan to accomplish, and then plan a review time to check on progress.

2. **Pomodoro Technique**—The Pomodoro Technique was invented in the early '90s by Francesco Cirillo and is named after the tomato-shaped kitchen timer. ("Pomodoro" means "tomato" in Italian.) Set the timer for a consistent block of time (traditionally it's twenty-five minutes, but who gets something done in twenty-five minutes? I set it for thirty to sixty minutes). Your goal is to focus on your task during that time. You should not check e-mail or social media or talk to or meet with someone during that time. When the timer goes off, you take a short break (traditionally five minutes) and then set the timer again to focus for another block of

PLAY

time. While this may not sound fun, if you find you have a hard time focusing, you will find yourself super happy when you see you are getting more done. To add more fun, you can do it with a buddy and check in at the start and on breaks.

3. **Set up a carrot**—What is something you can reward yourself with once you complete a task? Is it time with your partner, drinks, a night out with friends, a massage, a spa day, a vacation day, a dinner out? It has to be something you are very much looking forward to. Make a commitment that if you finish your task on time, you will reward yourself with that. To make it more fun, jointly create a reward that you can do together with a colleague. You can only celebrate the reward if both of you finish what you need to in the timeframe you committed.

NOW IT'S YOUR TURN

PLAY

When you take play more seriously, it's amazing what shifts in your culture. I invite you to implement these tips and "play" with these questions to foster a culture of play, first individually and then with your team. If you only have time to take on the **key questions** in each section, you will begin to develop a stronger culture of play in your organization.

HERE ARE SOME QUESTIONS TO SHIFT YOUR MIND-SET AROUND PLAY:

1. How could you relate to work as more fun?

2. What would you need to let go of or take on for that to be true?

3. Who would you need to be to have that come true?

HERE ARE SOME QUESTIONS AND TIPS TO FOSTER PLAY FOR YOU AND YOUR TEAM:

 1. How can you make mundane or intense tasks more fun to complete? (for example, get-it-done buddy, Pomodoro Technique, set up a carrot)?

 2. In what ways can you encourage your team to set time out to "play"? How might that impact the rest of their workday? What if your team went for a walk or a matinée or played miniature golf at lunch? It doesn't have to

PLAY

take hours—just enough to get out of "work" to be more creative?

3. How can you solve problems or hold one another accountable in ways that are more fun than what you do today (for example, problem/solutions swap, flip chart building, speed ideation)?

TIP: Get your team together to "brainstorm on play." Facilitate a discussion with your team to brainstorm on ways the team can foster a culture of play, especially when your projects get very intense. Here are some questions to kick-start the session:

a. What does play mean to us? How can we "play" with play?

b. How can we incorporate more play in our days and weeks?

c. What kinds of things can we do together to foster more play?

PLAY

HERE ARE SOME QUESTIONS AND TIPS TO ENHANCE YOUR WORK ENVIRONMENT WITH MORE PLAY:

1. What would it take to update your office to foster more play? What is one action you are willing to take to help foster creativity in your work environment?

2. What is one action your team is willing to take to foster more creativity and play in your environment?

TIP: Working in different areas can cause the senses to come alive. Explore working in different areas of the building, or get outside to stimulate new thinking.

TIP: Set up plants, color, visuals in your office space, or colored paper on top of your desk.

TIP: Hold your next team meeting at a café or an area of a nearby hotel or outside on a patio or nearby park.

I would love to hear how you've been able to implement more play in your culture. Join our LinkedIn community to share your experience, get your questions answered, and get support.

PLAY

JOIN OUR LINKEDIN COMMUNITY AT:
LinkedIn.com/groups/12309555

DOWNLOAD THE WORKSHEETS AND RESOURCES AT:
stoptalkingstartaskingresources.com

**PRACTICE MAKES PROGRESS.
ONE QUESTION AT A TIME.**

PLAY

PLAY IS SERIOUS BUSINESS. WHEN YOU TAKE IT SERIOUSLY, YOUR CULTURE WILL SHIFT IN UNIMAGINABLE WAYS.

JEANMARIESPEAKS.COM

CHAPTER

10

SHARED SUCCESS

CULTURE OF
SHARED SUCCESS

WHAT DOES SUCCESS MEAN TO YOU?

If you asked that question to each and every person on your team, you would get a different answer. Success is completely subjective, yet it is something we all desire.

As employees, we have our own definitions of success. The organization has its own definition and vision of success. The challenge is ensuring alignment between the employees' vision of success and the organization's vision so all are shooting for the same target. As the organization grows, that alignment becomes even more challenging to achieve.

As a leader, there are many ways to measure success. It can be measured by how well you lead, how well you develop your people, how well-liked you are by your team, the impact you and your team make within the organization and with your customers, and the list can go on. As leaders, we often define what success looks like to us and then we set out to achieve it. I invite you instead to consider this:

What if *you* do not determine your success? What if the people you lead determine your success?

If that was the case, how successful would you be?

Success is not just about the end results and the goals your team achieves. While those are critical to the bottom line of the organization, the other factors that are important are how the team comes together to achieve the results and what the aftermath is. I've been on plenty of projects in which we reached the results we set out in the client's eyes and the company's eyes, but there was a high price to pay given the long work hours and level of burnout. Is that success? If we look at the cost of the actual hours worked against the revenue of the project, the margins can appear dismal. Is that success?

If the people you lead determine your success, it's

important to consider all the factors that make up success: the project results, the bottom line, the team's experience, and the aftermath.

As a leader we need to balance all of those factors, and it's not easy.

Leadership, first and foremost, is an internal job. It requires knowing who you are, recognizing your strengths and areas for improvement, and being extremely aware of yourself, your team, and how best to inspire and motivate your team members. It's recognizing when to admit you have failed and taking full responsibility for your behaviors, your actions and your inactions.

Leadership is also an outside job. It requires understanding your team; understanding the dynamics of the organization's structure, people, and politics; having a clear vision; and ensuring your team is fully enrolled in that vision. It's being the one who opens up doors, breaks down barriers, and paves the way for the team to succeed.

Then there is the team you help grow and develop. You need to ensure your team members are engaged and empowered and valued and recognized. Whew! Between the internal and external job, that's a tall order to meet. Being a leader is one of the most challenging, rewarding, difficult, and exciting roles you can have in an organization. With all of the responsibilities you have, it's a wonder you can come up for air.

If the team you lead determines your success, how often do you stop and think about how you could make your team successful? Not because you have to but because you want to. I'm going to guess it's not as often as you would like. Not because you don't want to or you don't care, but because it's challenging to manage it all.

What if success wasn't about you?

> ## What if success was about making others successful?

That is what I refer to as "shared success."

In order to foster a culture of shared success, we have to be willing to forgo *me* to create the greater *we* even though it's in our human nature to be driven to look out for numero uno before we take care of someone else. It is an incredible feeling to know that someone has helped you become successful. But how often are we stepping up to provide that support to someone else?

It is a challenge to shift from a *me* to a *we* mentality, and it is often the cause of the greatest disconnect in our work cultures today. It not only impacts our level of compassion and empathy toward one another; it also impacts our level of aliveness, motivation, and happiness at work.

How can I make you successful?

Can you imagine if all the people on your team silently asked that question the next time they saw you or thought about you? How would that feel?

Think of one person on your team you enjoy working with, a person you respect and value. Someone who makes you smile when you think of him or her. Imagine that person is in front of you right now and you are thinking, *"How can I make you successful?"* What immediately comes to mind that you would want to do for that person?

Now, take a moment and think of one person you work with who is sometimes challenging—difficult or hard to be with. Imagine that person is right in front of you. Putting your past judgments about that person aside, ask yourself, *"How could I make you successful?"* What immediately comes up for you? What could you do for that person that you haven't done in the past? How could you act differently when you see him or her? What might that person most need right now?

Now, think of your own manager or the person you report to. All judgment aside, what if you looked at him or her and thought, *"How can I make you successful?"* If you took some time to sit with that question, how would you be different with your manager in the future? What might you do differently the next time you see him or her?

What you have just stepped through is the power of inquiry.

"How can I make you successful?" is a type of question called an inquiry.[17] It's not meant to be asked directly to another. It's a question you dwell in and answer yourself. Each time you ask it, you may get a different answer. An inquiry shifts your state of being in the moment. It helps provide a perspective to hold as you work with others. An inquiry can shift how you see them and work with them. Ultimately, an inquiry such as this can shift the entire culture of your organization—if you allow it to.

Imagine walking into work tomorrow, and all the people you work with are thinking in the back of their minds, "How can I make you successful today?" Your manager is thinking about how to make you successful, your team members are thinking about how to make you successful, and your peers and even your customers are wondering how they can make you successful.

How does that feel?

I'm gonna guess it feels pretty dang good!

How would your team members feel if you took that inquiry on for each of them? What if you looked at your department from the perspective of *"How can I make you successful?"* Now expand that perspective out to your manager, peers, customers, and clients.

What would be possible for you, them, and the organization if you came from that perspective?

What this inquiry does is it shifts us from *me* to *we*.

When we think back to the concept of tribes and the most primitive ways human beings grouped themselves together, there was no distinction between *me* and *we*.[18] The group took care of its members always and in all ways. The men went out to hunt. The women gathered. Each person utilized his or her gifts and talents to do what was needed to survive. Everything was handled.

This one inquiry—*"How can I make you successful?"*—requires you to put your ego and needs aside and help another. It may also mean having to compromise your own needs for the sake of the team, department, or organization. It requires trust and respect for one another despite disagreements. And it requires you to let go of judgments you may be carrying of others. Let's face it; we can be judging machines. What if, instead of judging, we practiced this inquiry and turned our judging machine into a highly supportive, well-oiled success engine?

Fostering a culture of shared success is about measuring the success of your leaders by how successful they make others.

When interviewing people for leadership positions, Mark C. Crowley, author of *Lead from the Heart*, challenges all hiring professionals and managers to ask the interviewees, "Tell me three people whose careers you personally helped promote and what did you do

SHARED SUCCESS

to invest in them."[19] If that interviewee cannot answer this question confidently, you may want to think twice about hiring that person.

If you focus on making others successful, success will come back tenfold. If you want to foster a culture of shared success, stop talking and start dwelling in the inquiry, *"How can I make you successful?"*

NOW IT'S YOUR TURN

 Experiment with this inquiry and key question, "How can I make you successful?"

HOW TO APPLY THE SUCCESS INQUIRY ON-THE-JOB:

1. **Prior to a one-on-one.** Just prior to having a one-on-one, ask the question, *"How can I make you successful?"* to yourself with the other person in mind and see what comes up. You may notice a shift in how you are with that person. You may even be inspired to help that person. Or it may shift you into a state of curiosity so that you are inspired to ask more questions about how the person is doing and what they most need.

2. **In a meeting.** When you are in a meeting with others, without being too obvious, pick a person in that meeting. With that person in mind, imagine asking the question, *"How can I make you successful?"* and see what comes up.

3. **With your manager or a member of your team or department.** Pick one person a day to apply the inquiry with. It could be your manager or someone from your team or department. How can you make them successful?

4. **With people you are challenged with.** Pick three people at work that you are currently challenged with, and with each of them in mind, apply the inquiry, *"How can I make you successful?"*

5. **With your customers.** Think of the customers you interact with. Pick one you have neglected lately. How can you make that customer successful? What is one action you could take on to help that customer be more successful?

If the only question you asked every day was this—"How can I make you successful?"—you would begin to shift the culture of your teams and ultimately your organization.

SHARED SUCCESS

If you want to be successful, help others become successful.

PRACTICE MAKES PROGRESS.
ONE QUESTION AT A TIME.

WHAT IF SUCCESS WAS ABOUT MAKING OTHERS SUCCESSFUL?

JEANMARIESPEAKS.COM

CHAPTER

11

UNSTOPPABILITY

CULTURE OF
UNSTOPPABILITY

WHAT DOES IT MEAN TO BE UNSTOPPABLE? It means taking action in the face of fear. It means doing what it takes to get the job done even if it's not in your job description. It means helping another out even when your plate is full because you know it's for the best interest of the organization.

It's going above and beyond the call of duty to resolve a customer issue. It's taking the initiative to resolve an issue before someone asks. It's stepping up and taking action when things aren't getting done. It's calling people out on their sh*t and not letting them get away with it because you care about what's best for the culture, not because you want to be recognized as a hero or savior.

It's about being the very best you can be and having the courage to stretch yourself beyond where you thought you could go. It's knowing that opportunities can arise in the face of challenges, downturns, low morale, or layoffs. It's knowing deep in your heart that you are here to make a difference. It's improving the organizations you work in and the communities that you live because you know there is something greater than you that is at play. It's understanding that we all live on the same planet, so if we all don't take care of it and of one another, we are all impacted.

> **In the end, it's having an unwavering commitment that is bigger than you and not allowing anyone or anything to get in the way of that.**

Nowhere in those statements did I mention being a bulldog or a bulldozer running over people so that you can achieve your goals. I did not mention being unstoppable at the cost of others. Being unstoppable is having a keen awareness and caring for all who are around you as you move forward.

Forward is the operative word here. The level of

action that takes place when you are unstoppable is often off the charts.

When I was twenty-six years old, I was four years into working at the high-tech startup, Cambridge Technology Partners. The company had just gone public. Prior to that, the venture capital firm had brought in a CEO and CFO from the outside. I had never officially met the CEO, but he seemed friendly at the time. He definitely didn't feel like "one of us" though. It was clear he was from the outside. He was very put together and "slick" in how he dressed and how he carried himself. He had executive presence.

I had just come off of a three-day weekend where I had attended a growth and development seminar that I had been referred to by a friend. I had wanted to understand more about my life purpose—and "what I'm here for"—so it was right up my alley. I knew it would be intense, but it was more than that. It rocked my world. It had me look at my past and how I had been acting and showing up in the world, and it inspired me to start taking responsibility for who I was so I could create the life I wanted. It was eye-opening for me. It was the first time I had done any kind of inner work. It was life altering.

I have no idea what got into me, but as soon as I went into work on the following Monday, I found myself on a mission. What immediately came to mind was this: "I have got to bring this experience I had into the company." I had gotten so much out of it that I wanted others to experience it and see what was possible for their work and life. I was still very private at work and not one to open up personally and share with people I didn't know, but there was a deep calling to do this.

Nothing was going to get in my way. I needed to tell the CEO how amazing this was and see if we could explore bringing it into the company. Having never met the CEO, I had no clue how to get access to him. At the time, he seemed so "high up" from those I was interacting with that I had no idea how to reach him.

Who knew that CEOs had executive assistants? I got that lowdown from a colleague, so I walked over to his assistant's cubicle and asked to be put in his calendar. Little ole me on the CEO's calendar. As soon as she clicked her mouse to secure the meeting, I could feel the sweat in my palms. I immediately thought, "What am I doing?" I thanked her and walked away from her cubicle acting "cool," but deep down inside, I was freaking out. What was I thinking? But there was another part of me that felt excitement. I was going to do this. Then I remembered a quote by Fritz Perls, MD and founder of Gestalt Therapy who said, "Fear is excitement without the breath."[20] Boy, was I feeling that.

Fast-forward a week later. I will never forget how nervous I was. Would I say the right thing? Was I dressed appropriately? Would I be articulate enough? Would he think I was way too "out there"? Would he turn down my idea? Would he think I was crazy?

But you know what? Those thoughts came in, and within a few minutes, they quickly left because I had a much bigger commitment for helping people and seeing what was possible for the company and the people in it. Nothing was going to stop me from having this meeting.

As I walk over to see his assistant, I could feel a rush of heat come over me. I had never had a meeting with a "CEO" before. She called him on the phone to let him know I was there and then pointed me to go into his office. I had never been in his office. I knew where it was because I could see it every time I went to the restroom, but all those times, I could only see the door.

I walked into this room that was the size of the entire floor of my apartment, and the first thing I thought of was *"Wow,* this is a big office!" Then, the next thing that came out of my mouth was *"Wow,* this is a big office!"

Yup, that's how I started the meeting. No introductions. No "Hi, how are you?" I just commented on how friggin' big the size of his office was. I honestly didn't think people had offices that big, and it really surprised me.

He motioned me to sit down in one of his "living room" chairs across from his large, shiny mahogany desk where he was sitting, and he said with a very warm and friendly demeanor, "What can I do for you?" With

UNSTOPPABILITY

sheer excitement, passion, and commitment, I shared my experiences at the seminar I had just taken, what I got out of the seminar, and what could be possible if we brought it into our company.

He listened intently, 100 percent present to what I was saying, and after I had shared my excitement, he said, "I think it's a great idea. Why don't you talk to the COO and figure out how to make it happen."

Whhhhaaat? I was beside myself. First of all, I had been talking with the CEO (in his big huge office). Then I had shared my crazy idea of bringing this "out there" seminar to our company. And he had said *yes*? Was this for real? I walked out of his office on cloud nine. I had done the thing I had never imagined I could do!

That experience boosted my confidence and re-minded me that when I was committed to something bigger than me, and I didn't let anything get in the way, I could make it happen. I was unstoppable.

Being unstoppable is having the fear and taking the action anyway. It's not letting your inner critic stop you in your tracks. It's listening to the unwavering commitment you have that is so much bigger than you and then taking action to make it happen.

> What would be possible if you
> were unstoppable?
> What would be possible if your team
> was unstoppable?

When you foster a culture of unstoppability, you and your team take on an unwavering commitment to go beyond what you thought was possible.

Imagine if all the teams and departments in your organization went above and beyond what they thought was possible. When you foster a culture of unstoppability, it creates a ripple effect. Once you initiate, it's contagious. The impact is not just within your team; it ripples out and impacts your clients and their communities. It starts with one leader at a time taking the initiative and having a passion and unwavering commitment that is bigger than the leader to inspire the team.

HOW DO WE BECOME UNSTOPPABLE?

I'm going to assume that you have team goals and targets and that you have a company mission and vision. But do you have a specific vision and mission for your team? What kind of difference do you and your team want to make in your organization, with your customers, and with those your customers serve? What's your bigger commitment that goes beyond any individual commitment you or your team has?

UNSTOPPABILITY

If you don't know what that is, I encourage you to take time with your team to brainstorm on what that would look like.

Once you are clear on what you are committed to, there is a powerful question and mind-set shift that can help you achieve your commitment without having you feel like you have to work harder. Let me explain. Let's say, for example, that you feel overwhelmed and have more on your plate than you can handle. In order to feel better, you take some time to write out your to-do list and then you take time to prioritize the list. Now you know what to do. But it still doesn't mean you will do it. It just means you are now more organized. The powerful question to ask next is this:

> ## "Who would you need to *be* to get all this done?"

I'm not looking for a person here like "Toni Robbins" or "your sister, who has a level of focus as sharp as a knife." The answer is a way of being; for example, you might need to be more patient or focused or confident or unstoppable.

When we focus, and I mean 100 percent focused on practicing *being* a particular way, it's amazing how much gets done, how many goals get met, and how much our vision comes true. All because we started out from a place of *being*.

Going back to the big list of items to tackle, if you took on *being* more patient as you went through your list of tasks, how do you think that would go? You would probably feel calmer and less anxious. You might be more precise and not let things slip through the cracks.

If, instead, you took on *being* focused, what would it be like to tackle the items? You might accomplish more in less time because you would not let yourself get distracted by social media or e-mail or whatever rings, buzzes, and pops up in the form of notifications.

If you took on *being* unstoppable as you tackled your list of items, there would be a different energy. When you take on being unstoppable, you are not only hyperfocused; there is also a level of "I'm going get this done come hell or high water." When you put your energy first on *being*, it informs the doing.

We are so used to focusing on the result that we go into "doing" mode right away. We don't stop to think about who we need to *be*. Even if we are procrastinating or avoiding, we are still "doing."

We are all born with an incredible ability to *be*, yet so little of us are leveraging it. When you tap into that power, achieving your results becomes surprisingly effortless and more fulfilling. This is why I believe we are called human "beings" and not human "doings".

Be first. Then *do.*

This is a powerful tool to apply to any goal or desire you have as a leader, for your team, or for your organization.

When you focus on *being* unstoppable as a leader, you will inherently challenge the status quo. You will help your team go to the edge of its comfort zone and beyond. When you are unstoppable, you will no longer tolerate gossip. Instead you will create a "no gossip" zone that ensures that if there is a complaint, it will come with a solution and be directed at the person who can do something about it. If your team members are frustrated that something does not exist and you focus on being unstoppable, you will inspire them to go create it or find out how to create it. When you are unstoppable, you take full responsibility for what you do and don't do, and you clean up when you mess up. You put your energy into making a difference. You are inspired to do all of this because you have taking on *being* unstoppable.

Unstoppability is moving from possibility to unwavering commitment. When you take on being unstoppable, there is no question in your mind that it's possible. You become an unwavering force that achieves your goals and desires.

When your team becomes unstoppable, it has a ripple effect throughout the organization. It is completely possible to create a culture of unstoppability.

One leader at a time. One team at a time.

NOW IT'S YOUR TURN

Fostering a culture of unstoppability takes initiative, passion, and an unwavering commitment. Ahead are questions and tools to help you and your team become unstoppable. Take a moment to review the sections and pick one section that is appropriate for your team to work on for a week. Even if you take on one question from one section, you will notice a shift. Less is more. If you only focus on the **key questions**, you will begin to develop a culture of unstoppability.

QUESTIONS TO UNCOVER A BIGGER COMMITMENT BEYOND YOU AND YOUR TEAM:

Key Questions for You As a Leader

 1. What would it take for you to *be* unstoppable? With your team, your manager, and the customers you serve? What would it take to inspire your team to be unstoppable?

2. What is the bigger commitment you have for your team and beyond? Are you living that commitment out? If not, what would it take?

217

With Your Team

 1. What is your mission and vision as a team? Who would you need to be to achieve your mission and vision?

2. What are you committed to as a team that has yet to be acted upon?

3. What kind of difference does your team want to make in your organization, with your customers, and with those they serve?

4. What does it mean as a team to be unstoppable?

QUESTIONS TO HELP YOU AND YOUR TEAM BECOME UNSTOPPABLE. PRACTICE MOVING FROM...

 1. "We can't do that" → "What's possible if?

 2. "That won't work" → "What if?

3. "Is this it?" → "How good could it get?"

4. "We failed" → "What if there was no such thing as failure?"

QUESTIONS TO ASK WHEN YOU OR YOUR TEAM FEELS STOPPED:

When you run up against an issue on your project or with your team, especially if you are unsure of which direction to take, experiment with one of these questions to shift out of the problem and move into possible solutions.

1. What else is possible?

2. What if we went in a different direction?

3. What if we looked at it differently?

4. What would be possible if we didn't do it this way?

5. What if we didn't know? What's possible from there?

6. What if it didn't matter?

7. What would it take to solve this issue?

As you dive into being unstoppable, I invite you to engage in our LinkedIn community to get support and learn how others are applying the questions and tools.

JOIN OUR LINKEDIN COMMUNITY AT:
LinkedIn.com/groups/12309555

DOWNLOAD THE WORKSHEETS AND RESOURCES AT:
stoptalkingstartaskingresources.com

UNSTOPPABILITY

Renaissance leaders are unstoppable. They lead with a different lens. They don't say, "Follow me; we are going this way." They ask, "What is possible and what will it take to get there?"

Dare to be unstoppable.

**PRACTICE MAKES PROGRESS.
ONE QUESTION AT A TIME.**

DARE TO BE UNSTOPPABLE.

JEANMARIESPEAKS.COM

IN CLOSING

CONGRATULATIONS!

You made it. Thank you for taking the time to make this a priority for you.

One of the things I learned in my early corporate days was this: The measure of success is not just what you learn. It's what you do with the learning afterward. When you apply the learning, you produce a result. The result may not be exactly what you hoped for, but it will always point you to greater learning. So, the important question now is:

> How will you apply the information you
> have just learned?

As you look at the state of your workplace culture, decide if it's best to focus on you, your team or your organization. Based on that, here is a quick reference to which chapters would most serve you and how:

DO YOU NEED TO FOCUS ON YOU?

- *Awareness* – Understand where you get stopped and how you can move forward faster.

- *Authenticity* – Be willing to tell the truth to yourself and express yourself fully.

- *Curiosity* – Practice judging less and staying more open to other's views and ideas.

- *Unstoppability* – Explore your bigger commitment and how to enroll your team in that.

DO YOU NEED TO FOCUS ON YOUR TEAM?

- *Accountability* – Help others be more accountable and responsible for their actions.

IN CLOSING

- *Acknowledgment* – Let your team members know how valuable they are.

- *Diversity* – Honor and respect all aspects your team brings to their work.

- *Authenticity* – Create the space for open, healthy and authentic communication on your team.

- *Play* – Create the time and space for more creativity and play.

- *Unstoppability* – Explore your team's bigger commitment and how to put it into action.

DO YOU NEED TO FOCUS ON YOUR ORGANIZATION?

- *Collaboration* – Explore collaborating with others outside of your team or department.

- *Learning* – Magnify and leverage the impact of your learning across the organization.

- *Shared Success* – Practice a mindset to help others become more successful.

IN CLOSING

I invite you to pick a chapter that would most serve you and reread it. Then try out the tips and questions in that chapter like a "Renaissance Detective." Practice shifting from "What am I going to say?" to "What question do I need to ask?"

JOIN OUR LINKEDIN COMMUNITY AT:
LinkedIn.com/groups/12309555

DOWNLOAD THE WORKSHEETS AND RESOURCES AT:
stoptalkingstartaskingresources.com

GET INFORMATION ON OUR MOBILE APP AT:
stoptalkingstartaskingapp.com

The beautiful gift we have as human beings is the capacity to shift how we see things, what we think, and what we do in every moment. Our brains are able to rewire, but we have to be willing to do what it takes to make the shift.

We have to be willing to ask new questions.

Questions engage the heart and mind of your team and help it make the shift from doing to being. When we stop talking and start asking, we open up the dialogue among our teams and colleagues and increase employee engagement, productivity, and happiness.

IN CLOSING

What would be possible if you started
asking more questions?

**HERE'S TO SHIFTING YOUR CULTURE
ONE QUESTION AT A TIME.**

IN CLOSING

ABOUT THE AUTHOR

JEAN MARIE DIGIOVANNA IS AN INTERNATIONAL KEYNOTE speaker, corporate educator, and Certified Executive Coach who is passionate about helping people think and lead differently. As one of the founding partners of Cambridge Technology Partners in 1991, she helped assimilate and train staff that grew from ninety people in Cambridge, Massachusetts, to more than 4,000 worldwide. She left in 1998 to start her consulting and coaching business where she inspires leaders and teams across the globe to impact the bottom line by improving communication, increasing employee engagement, and thinking innovatively.

Jean Marie has an insatiable appetite for learning, a childlike curiosity, and a natural gift for asking powerful questions. Her programs combine the tool of powerful questions with proven leadership strategies and techniques to create cultural transformation with her clients, who range from Fortune 500 companies to small businesses. Her programs are highly engaging and content-rich, with tools leaders and their teams can apply immediately to succeed.

In true renaissance spirit, when she isn't working, she is busy traveling the world, working in her art studio, skiing fast, or dancing to live Latin music.

Jean Marie partners with your organization or association to customize and deliver keynote speeches and Renaissance Leadership™ programs for experienced and emerging leaders. To learn more about her experiential keynote speeches and how her high-impact leadership programs could benefit your business, please visit her website at jeanmariespeaks.com.

THAT WHICH YOU SET OUT, DELIBERATELY CREATE AND BELIEVE IN WILL COME TO YOU. WITH STEADY FOCUS, A CLEAR MIND AND AN ACTIVE SPIRIT ANYTHING IS POSSIBLE.

JEANMARIESPEAKS.COM

ACKNOWLEDGMENTS

TO MY CLIENTS ACROSS THE GLOBE who open up to me with their challenges and trust me to support them, and from whom I learn something every single day in our work together: Thank you for being my teachers and for challenging me to grow beyond my comfort zone. Without you, the content in this book would not be possible.

To my book reviewers who took the time to review the chapters and provide candid and valuable feedback that pushed me to make the book even better. Thank you: Leah Carey, Andrea Mulligan, Jeffrey Deckman,

Bob Gleason, Karen Wall, Joe Nedder, Johanna Lyman, Maureen Ellenberger, Renay Picard, Di Cullen, and Suzandeise Puga.

To Polly Letofsky, my publishing coach, for keeping me on track, for supporting me every step of the way, and for believing in me. To Victoria Wolf, graphic and layout designer extraordinaire, for turning my ideas into reality. And to Tom Locke, my editor, for his attention to detail.

A special acknowledgment to Rachel Coburn Johnsen and Elizabeth Joy Mueller who kept me sane throughout the writing process and to Jeffrey Deckman who continued to remind me why I'm meant to do this work.

Last but never least, to my soul family, spirit guides and angels, God, and the universe, for helping me get out of my own way so I could be a clear channel to share these messages and tools with you, the reader.

With love & light,

Jean Marie

NOTES

[1]Whitworth, Laura, and Henry Kinsey-House, et al. *Co-Active Coaching: New Skills for Coaching People Toward Success in Work and Life.* Davies-Black Publishing, November 3, 1998.

[2]By Brant Ott, "A Performance Development Approach Works Because It Creates Individualized Accountability," Gallup Workplace, October 12, 2017, https://www.gallup.com/workplace/231620/why-performance-development-wins-workplace.aspx.

[3]Partners in Leadership, "The 3 Steps to Transforming Millennials into Powerhouses", Inc., May 24, 2017, https://www.inc.com/partners-in-leadership/the-3-steps-to-transforming-millennials-into-powerhouses.html.

[4]Larry Alton, "How Millennials are Reshaping What's Important in Corporate Culture," Forbes, June 20, 2017, https://www.forbes.com/sites/larryalton/2017/06/20/how-millennials-are-reshaping-whats-important-in-corporate-culture/#5b08a1ab2dfb.

[5]Judith E. Glaser, "Self-Expression", Psychology Today, February 15, 2016, https://www.psychologytoday.com/us/blog/conversational-intelligence/201602/self-expression.

[6]Dan Cable, Francesca Gino and Bradley Staats, "The Powerful Way Onboarding Can Encourage Authenticity," Harvard Business Review, November 26, 2015, https://hbr.org/2015/11/the-powerful-way-onboarding-can-encourage-authenticity.

[7]Katie, Byron, *Loving What Is: Four Questions That Can Change Your Life.* Three Rivers Press, December 23, 2003.

[8]Glaser, Judith E., *Conversational Intelligence: How Great Leaders Build Trust and Get Extraordinary Results.* Routledge, April 30, 2016.

[9]2006, The Yale Book of Quotations by Fred R. Shapiro, Section: John A. Shedd, Page 705, Yale University Press, New Haven. (Verified on paper)

[10]Engel, Susan, *The Hungry Mind: The Origins of Curiosity in Childhood.* Harvard University Press, February 26, 2018.

[11]Glaser, *Conversational Intelligence.*

[12]Thomas Oppong, "The Curious Brain (Why Curiosity is as Important as Intelligence," Medium: Thrive Global, March 17, 2018, https://medium.com/thrive-global/the-curious-brain-why-curiosity-is-as-important-as-intelligence-d41799cae42d.

[13]Hawk Newsome, "Reaching Your Enemy: Interview with Hawk Newsome," Black Lives Matter, October 10, 2017, https://www.youtube.com/watch?v=mp9nsc-vBTY&t=11s.

[14]Cable, Gino and Staats, "The Powerful Way Onboarding Can Encourage Authenticity."

[15] Rae Pica, "Why Kids Need Recess," Pathways to Family Wellness, March 1, 2010, https://pathwaystofamilywellness.org/Children-s-Health-Wellness/why-kids-need-recess.html.

[16] "21st CEO Survey: Than Anxious Optimist in the Corner Office," PriceWaterhouseCoopers, 2018, https://www.pwc.com/gx/en/ceo-survey/2018/pwc-ceo-survey-report-2018.pdf.

[17] Whitworth, Co-Active Coaching: New Skills for Coaching People Toward Success in Work and Life.

[18] Carol R. Ember, "Hunter-Gatherers (Foragers)," July 23, 2014, https://hraf.yale.edu/ehc/summaries/hunter-gatherers.

[19] Crowley, Mark C, Lead from the Heart: Transformational Leadership for the 21st Century. Balboa Press, July 11, 2011.

[20] Perls, F., Hefferline, R., and Goodman, P., Gestalt Therapy: Excitement and Growth in the Human Personality. Souvenir Press Ltd, 1995.